Keto Diet Recipes For Women Over 40

All Your Favorite, Delicious Keto Comfort Foods.

Table of Contents

Introduction 7

Chapter 1 13

What Is Keto Diet? 13

Chapter 2 23

Ketosis 23

Chapter 3 38

How Is Insulin Affected By The Keto Diet 38

Chapter 4 49

Positive And Negative Effect Of Keto Diets 49

Chapter 5 63

Mistakes in Keto diet...........**Errore. Il segnalibro non è definito.**

Chapter 7 101

Gentle Approach To Keto For Women Over 40 101

Chapter 8 117

Keto Diet For Longevity 117

Chapter 9 128

Exercise For Women Over 40 In Support Of Keto....128

Chapter 10 169

Understanding The Different Types Of Fats 169

Chapter 11 180

OMEGA-3-6-9 180

Chapter 12 193

    Fat Bombs 193

Chapter 13 197

    Keto Bread Homemade... 197

Chapter 14 203

    Keto Pizza 203

Chapter 15 208

    Keto Recipes.. 208

Conclusion 246

Introduction

Eating a healthy diet is not about rigid limits, being unrealistically slim, or depriving yourself of the food you want. It's about feeling great, having more time, enhancing your health, and boosting your attitude instead.

It does not have to be overly complicated to eat healthily. When you feel overwhelmed by all of the contrasting food and health recommendations out there, you're not alone. It seems you'll have someone claiming the exact opposite for every doctor who advises you a certain diet is perfect for you. The fact is that while it has been shown that certain particular foods or nutrients have a positive effect on mood, the most important thing is your overall dietary pattern. The foundation of a healthy diet should be to replace processed food whenever possible, with real food. Eating food that very close to nature as possible can make a huge difference in the way you think, look, and feel.

You can break through the mystery by using these simple tips, and learn how to create — and keep to — a delicious, balanced, and nutritious diet that is as good for your mind as it is for your health.

Eating healthy begins with great planning. If you have a well-reserved kitchen, a stash of quick and easy recipes, and plenty of healthy snacks, you will have won half the healthy diet battle.

One of the best ways to get a healthy diet is to regularly cook your food and eat in. Choose a few healthy recipes you and your family like, and create a meal schedule around them. If you're preparing three to four meals a week and enjoying the leftovers the other days, you'll be farther ahead than dining out or getting frozen dinners most nights.

Healthy eating ingredients are generally found around the outer edges of most grocery stores, while the central avenue is filled with processed and packaged foods that aren't good for you. Check the store's perimeter for most of your grocery stores and try to cook one or both weekend days or weekend evenings and add more to save or set aside for a different night.

Cooking ahead saves time and money, and it's gratifying to know you've got a home-cooked meal waiting for you to eat.

Challenge yourself to come up with one or two dinners that you can put together without going to the store using stuff in the pantry, freezer, and spice rack. A delicious, whole grain pasta dinner with a quick tomato sauce or a quick and easy black bean quesadilla on a whole-wheat flour tortilla (among endless other recipes) might act as your go-to meal when you're just too busy shopping or cooking.

Switching to a healthful diet doesn't have to be a proposition about everything or nothing. You don't have to be excellent, you don't have to eliminate foods that you enjoy completely, and you don't have to change everything at once, which usually only leads to cheating or giving up on your new food plan.

A good approach would be to make a few minor changes at a time. Maintaining modest goals can help you achieve more in the long run without feeling deprived or overwhelmed by a major diet overhaul. Think of planning a healthy diet as some small, manageable steps, such as adding one salad once a day to your diet. You can continue to increase more healthy choices as your little changes become a habit. So try just keeping things simple—no need to complicate eating a healthier diet. Of starters, rather than being overly concerned about counting calories, think about your food in terms of color, diversity, and freshness. Focus on refrain from packaged and processed foods and, where possible, opting for more fresh ingredients.

Many patients have recently been inquiring about a ketogenic diet. They all ask if it's safe? Or would you advise? Notwithstanding the recent hype, a ketogenic diet is not new. We have used it in medicine for nearly 100 years to treat drug-resistant epilepsy, particularly in children. Dr. Atkins popularized his very-low-carbohydrate diet in the 1970s for weight loss, which started with a very strict ketogenic phase of two weeks. Over the years, other fad diets have incorporated a similar weight loss approach.

We provide solid proof that a ketogenic diet eliminates children's epilepsy, sometimes just as much as drugs. Because of these neuroprotective effects, the possible benefits for other brain disorders such as Alzheimer's Parkinson's, Parkinson's, multiple sclerosis, sleep disorders, autism, and even brain cancer have been raised. There is no human thesis to support recommending ketosis for the treatment of these conditions, though.

Weight loss, however, is the primary reason patients take the ketogenic diet. Previous research shows good evidence of a faster weight loss compared to participants on a more traditional low-fat diet or even a Mediterranean diet when patients go on a ketogenic or very low-carbohydrate diet. However, over time, that difference in weight loss seems to vanish.

A ketogenic diet has also been shown to boost blood sugar control, at least in the short term, in people with type 2 diabetes. If we consider the effect on cholesterol levels, there is even more debate. Some studies show some patients, in the beginning, have an increase in cholesterol levels, only to see cholesterol fall a few months later. But there is no long-term research that analyzes its effects on diabetes and high cholesterol over time.

I will provide you with all the appropriate information in this eBook and my encounters when using the Keto diets for women over 40. You are entitled to read this book entirely because I did it for you. All my sleepless nights, long days of studying, many tests, and hypotheses are all for you to get something real to put your eye on and completely read it out. You have the right to throw yourself into all the information that you will immediately harness from it. It's your body, and nobody's supposed to tell you what you want. I'll share tangible information in this book to help you get weight loss. I'll teach you how to make use of Keto foods, all your favorite, delicious Keto comfort foods, and how to make them intensely at home.

I bet you are on the right track. I segmented the book into two interesting parts to make it easy to read and enable you to take full benefit of all the information you need.

Part 1

Chapter 1
What Is Keto Diet?

The ketogenic diet can be defined as a high-fat, low-carbohydrate diet, adequate-protein that is primarily used in medicine to treat children with difficult-to-control epilepsy. The diet is forcing the body to burn fats instead of carbohydrates.

The carbohydrates contained in food are normally converted into glucose, which is then transported around the body and is especially important in fueling brain function. However, if the diet still contains little carbohydrates, the liver converts fat into fatty acids and ketone bodies. The ketone bodies go into the brain, replacing glucose as a source of energy. A dignified level of ketone bodies in the blood, a condition known as ketosis, results in a reduction in epileptic seizure frequency. About half of epileptic children and young people who have tried some form of this diet have seen the amount of seizures drop by at least half, and the effect persists even after the diet is discontinued. Some proof suggests that adults with epilepsy may gain from the diet, and a less stringent diet such as a changed diet of Atkins is similarly effective. Potential side effects may include high cholesterol, constipation, slowing growth, acidosis, and kidney stones.

A ketogenic or ketogenic diet is a low-carb, mild, high-fat protein diet that can help you burn fat more efficiently. It has lots of advantages for weight loss, health, and performance. These Keto diets have been highly recommended by so many doctors, particularly useful for losing excess body fat without hunger and improving type 2 diabetes. Therefore, while eating far fewer carbohydrates on a keto diet, you maintain moderate protein intake levels and may increase your fat intake. Reducing carb intake puts your body in a metabolic state known as ketosis, where you use energy to burn fat out of your diet and body.

Before I drive you deeper, what exactly does the term "keto" mean

The "keto" in a ketogenic diet appears from the fact that it permits the body to generate small fuel molecules called "ketones." This is another source of fuel for the body, which is used when there is a shortage of blood sugar (glucose).

The liver produces ketones from fat when you eat very few carbs or very few calories. These ketones then act as a source of fuel for the entire body, particularly for the brain.

The brain is a hungry organ which uses up a lot of energy every day, and can not run directly on fat—only glucose-or ketones-can run.

On a ketogenic diet, all of the body changes the supply of fuel to work mostly on carbohydrates, burning fat 24-7. The fat burning can increase dramatically when insulin levels become very low. Burning them off is making it easier to access your fat stores.

This is fantastic if you're trying to lose weight, but there may also be other, less obvious benefits, such as less appetite and a constant supply of energy (we can get from high carb meals without the sugar peaks and valleys). This can help to keep you alert and centered. It enters a metabolic state called ketosis when your body produces ketones. The speedy way to get there is by fasting— not eating anything— but no one can ever run reliably.

On the other hand, a keto diet also leads to ketosis and can be eaten continually. It has an amount of the advantages of fasting without having to fast long-term, including weight loss.

The keto diet emphasizes weight loss by the burning of fat. The goal is to lose weight quickly and ultimately feel more with fewer cravings while boosting your mood, mental focus, and energy. According to the keto proponents, you enter a state of ketosis safely by slashing the carbs you use up and instead filling up on fats. That is when both dietary and stored body fat breaks down into substances called ketones. Your fat-burning system now relies primarily on fat for energy–rather than sugar. Although similar in some ways to familiar low-carb diets, the extreme carb constraints of the keto diet–about 20 net carbs a day or less, depending on the version–and the deliberate shift to ketosis are what distinguish this increasingly popular diet. Other eating plans pull in keto elements, so you can find forms like eco-keto and at least one commercial diet that includes keto-friendly products.

The keto diet has its ancestry in the decades-old ketogenic therapeutic diet. Clinically, the ketogenic diet is used in medical treatment, most commonly for reducing epilepsy in infants that are hard to control.

Previously, an Italian professor of surgery, Dr. Gianfranco Cappello of Sapienza University in Rome, presented the diet as a weight-loss diet. Around 19,000 dieters have received a high-fat liquid diet through a feeding tube inserted down the nose in his 2012 study. The study showed a mean weight loss in participants of more than 20 pounds, most of whom retained it off for at least a year. The investigators reported some minor side effects, such as fatigue.

The healthcare community takes note of the high public interest in keto. Most people feel less hungry about the high-fat keto diet, and their overall calorie consumption will decrease. Besides weight loss, there was good news for diabetes management, with early, still-going research enhancing insulin sensitivity and blood-sugar regulation for individuals adopting a ketogenic diet.

How does Keto Diet work?

You can stay on a keto diet indefinitely, do it as a weight-loss plan for a short time or cycle in and out. Fat-rich foods are key, proteins are moderate, and carbs are bad guys.

Some tips to get started on keto:

• Educating yourself about carbs and getting to know good fats is the first step.

• Before you jump in, experiment with low-carb vegetables in the natural products section of the grocery store, find sources of grass-fed meat, and learn about hidden sources of sugar, such as coleslaw in your local food store.

• Don't believe that the sugar cravings will disappear immediately. Alternatively, make keto-friendly sweets like dark chocolate and nut butter.

• During the first week of carb retraction, you may experience symptoms such as muscle aches, headaches, fatigue, and mental turmoil–and, yes, hunger. Try bite on a high-fat snack like a bacon strip or some avocado mayonnaise cucumber for early cravings.

As the diet moves into the third and fourth weeks, you'll start to feel better. Soon, low-carb, high-fat food will seem more normal as it becomes an obsession. By week four, you can anticipate weight loss, particularly if you've been physically active while keeping a close eye on the plan.

Choosing the right food will be easier as you get used to the keto approach. Instead of lean meats, the emphasis is on skin-on food, fatter sections such as chicken thighs, rib-eye steaks, grass-fed ground beef, fatter fish such as tuna, beef brisket or bacon, and pork shoulder. Leafy greens, for instance, lettuce, spinach, and kale, as well as broccoli, cauliflower, and cucumbers, make healthy choices but avoid starchy root foods such as carrots, potatoes, turnips, and parsnips.

Oils such as avocado, olive, canola, linseed, and palm, as well as mayonnaise, will taste the salads while they are fattened. Clarified butter, or ghee, is a fat that you use to cook or spread.

Start your day with almond butter-boosted latte, coffee or tea, or have bacon and eggs as a simple breakfast. Stick with whole-grain milk, cheese, and other whole-grain milk products. Use stevia as a substitute for sugar and artificial sweeteners.

On the other side, fat makes up 70 to 73% of the daily diet. Protein fills out the meal plans, consisting of a modest one-fifth to one-quarter breakfast, lunch, and dinner regular, along with one or two suggested snacks. (Carb/fat/protein amount vary from diet to diet with each author.) For perpetuation over time, Vogel suggests taking a cyclical approach and entering and leaving ketosis, especially for women.

Dieters use some signs to know that they are in ketosis, some more subjective than others. Easy DIY urine or blood test results, poor or fruity breathing, decreased appetite, better mental focus, improvements in exercise performance, and weight loss can all suggest ketosis.

Keto risks

A ketogenic diet poses many risks. Top of the list: Saturated fat is high. Due to the link to heart disease, experts recommends that you keep saturated fats to no more than 7 percent of your everyday calories. And indeed, the keto diet is related to an increase in "poor" LDL cholesterol, which is also associated with heart disease.

Other potential keto risks include these:

Nutrient deficiency. "If you don't take a large variety of vegetables, fruits, and grains, you can run the risk of micronutrient deficiencies, including selenium, magnesium, phosphorus, and vitamins B and C,".

The problems with the liver. With so much fat to assimilate, the diet may aggravate any existing liver conditions.

Kidney problems. The kidneys help to assimilate protein, and the keto diet may overload them. (Currently recommended protein intake averages 46 grams per day for women and 56 grams per day for men).

Constipation. The keto diet is little in fibrous foods such as cereals and legumes.

Fuzzy thinking and mood swings. "To function, the brain needs sugar from healthy carbohydrates. Low-carb diets can cause confusion and irritability,"

These risks add up — so make sure you talk to a physician and a registered dietitian before you ever try a ketogenic diet.

Chapter 2

Ketosis

Ketosis is a metabolic state where fat supports the greater part of the body's fuel. It happens when access to glucose (blood sugar) is limited, which is the preferred source of fuel for many cells in the body. Most often associated with diets that are ketogenic and very low in carb. It also happens during pregnancy, in infancy, fasting, and hunger.

In general, people need to eat less than 40 grams of carbs per day and sometimes as little as 20 grams per day to get into ketosis, and this requires taking off certain food part from your diets, such as candy, grains, and soft drinks. You have to cut legumes, potatoes, and fruit, too.

Hormone insulin levels go down when eating a very low-carb diet, and fatty acids are released in large amounts from body fat stores. Many of these fatty acids are moved to the liver, oxidizing them and turning them into ketones (or ketone bodies). Those molecules could provide the body with energy.

Unlike fatty acids, ketones in the absence of glucose can cross the blood-brain barrier and provide energy for the brain. Without dietary carbs, the brain does not function as a common misunderstanding. True, glucose is preferred, and there are certain cells in the brain that can only use glucose for fuel.

A large portion of your brain, however, can also use ketones for energy, for example, during hunger or when your diet is low in carbs.

In reality, the brain gets 25 percent of its energy from ketones after just three days of starvation. This number rises to around 60 percent during long-term starvation. Additionally, during ketosis, your body may use protein to produce the little glucose that the brain still needs. That process is known as gluconeogenesis. Ketosis and gluconeogenesis are perfectly able to satisfy the energy needs of the brain. So if the brain doesn't get enough glucose, then it can use ketones for energy. The small amount of glucose that it still requires will come from protein.

In normal circumstances, glucose is used as their primary form of energy by body cells. People can get glucose typically from dietary carbs, including sugars and starchy foods. The body breaks down these into pure sugars. Afterward, it either makes use of glucose as fuel or stores it as glycogen in the liver and muscles. If there is insufficient glucose available to provide sufficient energy, the body will adopt an alternative strategy for meeting those needs. Specifically, it starts breaking down fat stores and using triglyceride glucose.

Ketones represent a by-product of this process. Such acids build up in the blood and leave the urine behind the body. We suggest the body breaks down fat in small amounts. High levels of ketones can, however, kill the body, resulting in a condition called ketoacidosis.

Ketosis assign to the metabolic state in which fat stores are converted into energy by the body, releasing ketones during the process.

All of these theories, I believe, have sunk well. Ok, let's see diabetes and ketosis.

Ketosis and diabetes

Ketosis may occur in people with diabetes due to a person who doesn't have enough insulin series of action glucose in the body. The appearance of ketones in the urine indicates a person needs to work on better diabetes control.

For people with type 2 diabetes, some dietitians recommend a keto diet. The body still produces some insulin with this condition, but it does not function as effectively. The keto diet aims to reduce a person's dietary carbs intake. Those with type 2 diabetes should aim to consume fewer carbs, as they convert to glucose and raise blood sugar.

Is Ketosis the Same as Ketoacidosis?

Ketosis and ketoacidosis are often confused. In a moment, I'll explain to you its differences.

While ketosis is a part of normal metabolism, ketoacidosis is a dangerous metabolic condition that, if left untreated, can be fatal. In ketoacidosis, excessively high levels of glucose (blood sugar) and ketones flood the bloodstream. The blood becomes acidic when this happens, which is seriously dangerous. Ketoacidosis is most often befriend with type 1 diabetes, which is not controlled. Although this is less common, it can also occur in people with type 2 diabetes.

Furthermore, severe alcohol dependence can lead to ketoacidosis. Ketosis is a normal metabolic state, whereas ketoacidosis is the most commonly seen serious medical condition in uncontrolled type 1 diabetes.

Its effects on Epilepsy.

Epilepsy is a cerebral disorder characterized by repeated seizures. It is a very common neurological condition that affects about 70 million people around the world. Anti-seizure medications can help control seizures in most patients. Nonetheless, about 30 percent of patients still have seizures despite using these medicines.

In the 1920s, the ketogenic diet was brought in people who don't respond to drug treatment as a treatment for epilepsy.

It has been used primarily in children, with some studies showing notable benefits. Most epileptic children on a ketogenic diet have experienced massive decreases in seizures, and some have even seen complete remission. Ketogenic diets can effectively reduce epileptic seizures, particularly in children with epilepsy who are not responding to conventional treatment.

Its effect on weight loss.

The ketogenic diet is a popular, science-supported, weight loss diet. Studies have found that ketogenic diets result in far greater weight loss than diets that are low in fat. One study reported weight loss for people on a ketogenic diet 2.2 times greater than those on a low-fat, calorie-restricted diet.

What's more, a ketogenic diet attributed to ketosis tends to make people feel less hungry and fuller. For this reason, calories are usually not expected to be counted on this diet. Studies show that ketogenic diets influence to greater weight loss compared with low-fat diets. Moreover, humans feel less hungry and more fuller.

Other Health Benefits of Ketosis

Ketosis and ketogenic diets may have additional therapeutic effects, too. These are now being tested as a treatment for a wide range of conditions:

- **Heart disease:** lowering carbohydrates to get ketosis can increase risk factors for heart disease such as blood triglycerides, total cholesterol, and HDL cholesterol.
- **Type 2 diabetes:** The diet may increase insulin sensitivity by up to 75%, and some people with diabetes may be able to reduce or even stop diabetes medicines.
- **Metabolic syndrome:** ketogenic diets can make better all major metabolic syndrome

symptoms, including high triglycerides, excess belly fat, and increased blood pressure.

- **Alzheimer's disease:** A ketogenic diet could benefit Alzheimer's patients.
- **Cancer:** Some analysis suggests that ketogenic diets can be helpful in cancer therapy, possibly by helping to "starve" glucose cells.
- **Parkinson's disease:** A small study found Parkinson's symptoms improved after 28 days of a ketogenic diet.
- **Acne:** There is some testify that this diet could reduce acne severity and progression.

Does ketosis have any negative effects on health?

You may experience some potential side effects from ketogenic diets and ketosis. These include headache, tiredness, constipation, high cholesterol, and poor breath. Most of the symptoms, however, are temporary and should disappear in a few days or weeks.

Additionally, some children with epilepsy developed kidney stones on a diet. And although extremely rare, there were a few cases of breastfeeding women who were likely to develop ketoacidosis caused by a low-carb or ketogenic diet.

Some people refer to this as "keto flu," although this is not an official medical condition. Drinking plenty of water can make those symptoms easier or help you avoid them.

People who take drugs that lower blood sugar should consult with a doctor before they try a ketogenic diet because the diet may decrease the need for medication. Ketogenic diets are sometimes low in fiber. For this reason, making sure you eat plenty of high-fiber, a low-carb vegetable is a good idea.

All that being said, ketosis is usually safe for the well. Yet it won't suit everyone. Many people in ketosis may feel great and full of energy, while others may feel miserable.

So Ketosis is a popular strategy for weight-loss. Low-carb eating plans involve the first part of the Atkins diet and the Paleo diet that stresses your body's proteins for fueling. Ketosis can help you burn fat, as well as make you feel less hungry. It also helps keep your muscles going.

Ketosis usually kicks in for healthy people who don't have diabetes and are not pregnant after 3 or 4 days of consuming less than 40 grams of carbohydrates a day. That's about three slices of bread, a cup of yogurt with low-fat fruit, or two small bananas. You can also start ketosis by fasting.

Test Your Ketones

By experimenting for ketones in your blood or urine, you can find out how much ketosis happens in your body. You don't need to go to a physician. You can buy the test strips at home to check your pee. Some ketones in your blood can be measured by blood sugar meters.

If you don't know how to test your ketones and when to speak with your doctor or diabetes instructor, high ketone concentrations are dangerous.

Tips to get in ketosis.

There are some ways to safely and effectively get into nutritional ketosis.

1. Reduce daily net carb intake to less than 20 grams: Eating less than 20 grams of net carbs each day virtually guarantees that you will achieve nutritional ketosis, although it is possible that you may not need to be this strict. What's like 20 grams of carb? Use our visual guide to find out or just try out our keto recipes and meal plans, limiting carbs to less than 20 grams per day.

2. Try intermittent fasting: Going without food for 16-18 hours may help you get faster into ketosis. Simply skip breakfast or dinner, which can feel very natural on an appetite-suppressing keto diet, makes this easy to do.

3. Don't be afraid of fat: Eating plenty of fat is an essential and delicious part of ketogenic food! Make sure each meal includes a source of healthy fat.

4. Cook with coconut oil: Besides being a natural fat that remains stable at high temperatures, coconut oil contains medium-chain fatty acids that can improve the production of ketone and can also have other benefits.

5. Exercise, if possible: You might not have enough time to participate in intense physical activity during the transformation into ketosis. Simply going for a brisk walk will, however, help you get more quickly into ketosis.

What is optimal ketosis?

Keeping ketogenic on a ketogenic diet isn't a black or white matter. It's not like you're in or out of ketosis. You can achieve various degrees of ketosis, instead. Defining my "optimal" ketosis varies according to your goals. For example, treating seizures may require a higher ketone level, where the degree of elevation may be less dependent than losing weight or raising blood sugar. This diagram shows that visually.

- Below 0.5 mmol / l is not acknowledged as a "ketosis," although a value of, say, 0.2 shows you are coming close. You may not be on your maximum fat-burning zone at this level.

- Nutritional ketosis occurs between 0.5-3 mmol / l. You would get a good effect on your weight and changes in metabolism.

- Some people call "optimal" ketosis about 1.5-3 mmol / l. However, the concept of optimal ketosis is controversial, and it is unclear whether it offers any substantial advantages over level 0.5-1.5. Exceptions could be to treat seizures or those who are interested in maximum gains in mental and physical performance.

- More than three mmol / l higher than required. Probably, it will achieve no better or worse results than at level 1.5–3.

Sometimes higher numbers can also mean you don't get enough food ("starvation ketosis").

In people with type 1 diabetes, ketone levels above 3.0 mmol / L may be caused by a severe insulin shortage, which requires urgent medical care.

- Over 8–10 mmol / l: Simply eating a keto diet is normally impossible to achieve this level. That means something is wrong. By far, the most common cause is type 1 diabetes, with severe insulin shortages. Symptoms include a very sick feeling of nausea, vomiting, abdominal pain, and confusion. The potential result, ketoacidosis, may be fatal and will require immediate medical attention.

Signs that you are in ketosis

Several signs suggest you are in ketosis, although the only objective way to verify it is to measure your ketones. Here are the most common ones:

- Dry mouth in the mouth or a metallic taste.
- Greater hunger, and more frequent urination.
- Keto breath' or' fruity breath,' which may be more apparent to others than you might.

- Initial tiredness, followed by increased energy.
- Increased appetite and food intake (one of the more positive side effects!).

Chapter 3
How Is Insulin Affected By The Keto Diet

Nutritional ketosis and diabetic ketoacidosis are conditions which are completely different. While nutritional ketosis is health-proof and beneficial, ketoacidosis is a medical emergency.

Alas, many healthcare professionals don't understand the difference between the two.

Ketoacidosis occurs primarily in people with type 1 diabetes unless they take insulin. Blood sugar and ketones rise to dangerous levels in diabetic ketoacidosis (DKA), which disrupts the delicate acid-base balance of the blood. Most ketoacidosis patients feel extremely ill and experience deep dehydration, vomiting, abdominal pain, and weakness. DKA requires hospitalization so you can administer IV fluids and insulin to lower your blood sugar gradually and safely.

The BHB levels typically remain below five mmol / L in nutritional ketosis. In diabetic ketoacidosis, however, people often have BHB levels of 10 mmol /

L or higher, which are directly related to their inability to produce insulin. This graph shows the vast difference between ketosis and ketoacidosis in the blood for ketones: When blood ketone elevate above a certain level, a pancreas capable of making insulin releases enough to shut down further ketone production. On the other hand, an individual with type 1 diabetes cannot make insulin by the pancreas. So ketones will continue to rise to life-threatening levels unless insulin is given through injection or IV.

Other people who may potentially get ketoacidosis are those with type 2 diabetes who are taking medicines known as SGLT2 inhibitors, such as Invokana, Farxiga, or Jardiance.

Besides, women who do not have diabetes may develop ketoacidosis during breastfeeding, in rare cases. However, it is almost impossible for most people capable of producing insulin to get into ketoacidosis.

A newly released study, the keto diet to be a game-changer or a lifesaver, raises questions about its capability to cause type 2 diabetes. The keto diet is a low-carbon, high-fat diet plan that causes a process known as ketosis to burn fat instead of carbohydrates. This is said to aid in weight loss.

However, keto diets don't allow the body to use insulin properly, so blood sugar isn't properly controlled. This results in insulin resistance, which can increase the risk of type 2 diabetes. "While ketogenic diets are known to be healthy, there are indications that there may be an additional risk of insulin resistance with this type of diet that may lead to type 2 diabetes A ketogenic diet may help some people with type 2 diabetes, as it allows the body to maintain low but healthy glucose levels.

The lower dietary intake of carbohydrates will help eliminate large spikes in blood sugar, thus reducing insulin requirement.

Studies on ketogenic diets, including research from 2018, found they could be useful in controlling HbAlc levels. This refers to the amount of hemoglobin-traveling glucose in the blood over approximately three months.

Ketogenic diets can help in lowering blood sugar levels. As such, some individuals with type 2 diabetes who also follow a ketogenic diet may be able to reduce their medication needs. However, those following the ketogenic diet may have a higher risk of developing hypoglycemia (low blood sugar) alongside an insulin regimen. Hypoglycemia occurs when blood sugar levels drop to or below 70 milligrams per deciliter (mg / dL).

It's good to have a discussion with your doctor about any diet changes while on the drug. Not consuming enough carbohydrates when taking certain diabetes medications can be dangerous.

If you want to do keto work for you, it helps you understand a little bit how the diet does its magic—and one of the big players here is the insulin hormone. Insulin does a lot of different things, but it's best known as the hormone you make for the metabolization of carbs.

Insulin gets a bad rap in low-carb circles, so much so that it can become oversimplified. Weight gain more than insulin! Insulin isn't necessarily bad for general health, and it's necessary for some health-related purpose (for example, if you want to acquire muscle, insulin is your friend for sure). Keto is not, however, merely about general health. Keto is about a specific shift in metabolism. If your specific goal is ketosis, then insulin is bad news.

The whole aim of the ketogenic diet is that instead of fat and carbohydrates, you are forcing your body to exploit ketone bodies for energy. That's what the diet does work.

Insulin reduces ketone production.

So if you need to get into ketosis and remain there, you want to minimize as much insulin as you can. The easiest method to do that is by changing what you eat unless you take insulin outside. Insulin is produced in response to various foods, so you can minimize the insulin production by changing your diet. That is what a ketogenic diet is all about.

Eating for low insulin production.

By restricting both carbs and protein, the ketogenic diet minimizes insulin production–the diet keeps carbs as low as possible and provides just enough protein to meet your needs, but no more.

To reduce insulin production, lower carbs

Carbs increase the insulin levels because insulin is needed to metabolize carbs (use them for energy). The more carbs you eat, the greater you need insulin. This works like this: Glucose (carbohydrate) in that food increases your blood sugar when you eat something carb-heavy. But to have high blood sugar all the time is hazardous, so when your body senses you have eaten carbohydrates, your pancreas makes some insulin to take that glucose out of the bloodstream and store it for later use in a safe place (your fat cells).

This is all fine and good, and you want it to work exactly like that if you're going to eat carbs. When you eat carbs but are unable to generate enough insulin (e.g., people with type 1 diabetes), you will find yourself in a very deep problem. But the flip aspect of this is that you have to lower carbs if you want to reduce the insulin production.

To reduce insulin production, lower protein

This one is more of a surprise–most people know that insulin has something to do with carbs, but not many people know that protein can trigger an insulin spike as well. Yet that's true!

The addition of whey protein to a mixed meal, for example, increased insulin response to the meal. Other types of milk protein are also insulinogenic– that is why keto focuses on high-fat, low-protein dairy foods (such as butter), not high-protein, low-fat dairy foods (such as Greek yogurts). It is all about reducing the spike in insulin.

How protein causes, this insulin response isn't entirely clear. Protein can cause a spike of insulin by stimulating the secretion of another protein, GLP-1, which then stimulates the secretion of insulin.

What is clear is that if you need a diet that reduces the production of insulin, you would like to reduce protein, too. In practice, getting protein down to just about nothing, the way you can with carbs, is not practical or even desirable. Protein does more than just cause spikes in insulin, and protein deficiency is causing its problems. So on keto, the goal is to get adequate protein: enough to keep you healthy and satisfy all your needs, but no more.

Keto: low in carbs, moderate in protein.

All this research on carbs, protein, and insulin explains why and how well you're getting keto. If the aim is to use ketones for energy, you have to reduce the production of insulin, which means minimizing carbs, reducing protein by quite a bit and relying on fat for calories for the most part, because fat is what you left. Fat raises the insulin stage very minimally, especially if it is not in an overeating context. A high-fat, adequate-protein low-carb diet does not completely prevent the production of insulin, but it reduces it by enough that the very low insulin content left does not stop you from making ketone bodies.

And the results are quite stunning. Eating a keto diet necessarily reduces fasting insulin and postprandial insulin (the levels of insulin immediately after a meal). A ketogenic diet minimizes the need for insulin in patients with diabetes who rely on outside insulin.

Keto, Resistance to insulin, and Sensitivity to insulin.

On the subject of keto and insulin, in general, it is worth noting how keto affects insulin sensitivity and resistance to insulin. Insulin gets glucose from your bloodstream (where it is hazardous) and into your muscles, liver, and fat tissue (where it is not). But to do that effectively, insulin needs to be able to "persuade" all of these issues to let the glucose in.

These other tendons are receptive to the insulin signal in people who are insulin sensitive: when insulin comes knocking, they're happy to open the door.

Those tissues resist the insulin signal in people who are insulin resistant. If insulin can not do its job, all that glucose stays right in the bloodstream (after all, where else will it go?), and the insulin-resistant person ends up getting high blood sugar all the time. It's called type 2 diabetes when this is diagnosed as an actual disease.

Now, look at what happens when a keto diet is thrown into that mix. Control of blood sugar improves, and people can reduce the amount of insulin they need to take as medication. This is particularly true for beginners with people with higher blood sugar. Keto is impressively effective for people with insulin resistance and blood sugar control problems–it also works for a female with polycystic ovary syndrome (PCOS), another condition characterized by insulin resistance, in addition to people with type 2 diabetes. Because a keto diet doesn't require that you be able to make or use insulin normally, it's very therapeutic for people who can't do that.

Knowing how and why a diet can help you put it into practice in your own life. If you just anticipate of keto as "low-carb," for example, you might be desirous of using a lot of whey protein powder, because people know that protein is the perfect macronutrient that makes you thin, right? But whey protein is, in fact, very highly insulinogenic, so it's not a great keto option!

By reducing protein as well as carbs, a ketogenic diet minimizes insulin–that's how it takes the brakes off ketone production and allows you to hop on the ketosis train.

Chapter 4
Positive And Negative Effect Of Keto Diets

The keto diet is again an eating plan that focuses on foods that provide plenty of healthy fats, enough protein, and very few carbohydrates. The goal is to gain more calories from the fat than from the carbohydrates.

The diet functions by depleting the body of its reserves of sugar. As a consequence, fat for energy will start to break down. This results in the production of ketones called molecules that the body uses for fuel. This can also lead to weight loss when the body consumes fats.

Several types of a keto diet are available, including Standard Ketogenic Diet and Cyclical Ketogenic Diet.

So I'll explain the benefit of Keto diets and the detrimental factors.

1. Support Weight Loss.

The ketogenic diet can help to improve weight loss in several ways, including metabolism boosting and appetite reduction. Ketogenic diets are foods that fill a person up, and that can reduce the hormones that stimulate hunger. For these reasons, a keto diet may lower the appetite and encourage weight loss.

Researchers found that, in a 2013 meta-analysis of 13 separate randomized controlled trials, people following ketogenic diets lost 2 pounds (lbs) more than those following low-fat diets over one year. Likewise, another study of 11 studies showed people losing 5 lbs more after a ketogenic diet than folks after six months of low-fat diets.

In a normal diet, carbohydrates are burned to your body for energy. If you restrict carbohydrates, though, your body will start burning fat instead of energy use. This means you'll lose body fat faster. Furthermore, the Keto diet's strategy of growing high-fat foods will help eliminate hunger cravings and feelings.

2. May Enhance Cognitive Function.

For a long time, the ketogenic diet was understood to affect brain function. The high-fat content in the diet helps reduce inflammation that causes nerve pain in the brain, and research shows that fewer migraines are encountered by overweight patients who go on a diet than before.

Studies are also tentative that diet may reduce symptoms or hinder the development of neurological diseases such as Alzheimer's and Parkinson's, and dietary children often show better attention and fewer symptoms of ADHD than their peers. Further attest shows that powering the brain on ketones after traumatic brain injuries can improve the outcome, although most research today has only looked at rat populations.

3. May Slow Different Cancers.

Evidence shows that a keto diet may slow tumor cell spread and even completely suppress its growth.

4. May Reduce Inflammation From High Blood Sugar;

The ketogenic diet helps lower your insulin levels, thus preventing it from triggering various health issues. There's also evidence that the diet will reduce your overall insulin sensitivity, making it easier for your body to process carbohydrates efficiently.

5. It Helps You to Kick The Habit of Sugar.

Obsession with sugar is a serious problem for millions of people, but it can make it easier to fight off cravings following the ketogenic diet because every meal leaves you satiated. Because the diet limits your intake of carbohydrates to 25 grams per day, you will cut your intake of sugar down to almost nothing, making it easier to quit the habit altogether.

6. May Increase Female Fertility.

More than 10 percent of American women struggle to conceive or carry a pregnancy to a term less than 44. Some notice that after the ketogenic diet, some of the underlying fertility issues seem to be improving. The eating plan positively influences weight and insulin levels, and it can mitigate the hormonal effects of polycystic ovarian syndrome (PCOS) Keto promises quick results (4–6 weeks), very nutritious diet, promotes more exercises, but they can be costly purchasing the products, not very reliable in the past few months, can have a severe lack of fiber in diet if performed Cons improperly.

Neither diet is flawless and has its share of downsides in the ketogenic diet.

1. Initial weight loss is mostly water.

It's not uncommon to experience breathtaking weight loss when you first go keto, but for many, these losses can't be maintained, and they rarely last. These initial losses are attributed primarily to the weight of the water from burning your glycogen stores. If you replenish your diet with carbs, some of those pounds will return.

2. Long-term Limited Research.

Despite the popularity of the diet today, the effects of a Ketogenic diet on your health over time are little known. This leaves analysts with more questions than answers about its effectiveness after years or decades of commitment. There is no conclusive attest as to whether Ketogenic practitioners can recover weight or experience any health consequences, which suggests that you may be at risk in the future if you practice the eating strategy today.

3. The Diet May Trigger Brain Fog.

Your brain is prepared to run on glucose and can affect your mental function by limiting this supply. This is because your body is struggling to make its transition from using an available energy supply, which can affect brain functioning in ways that lead to memory loss, headaches, slower cognition, and general' brain fog.'

Such symptoms are usually temporary and dissipate instead, as soon as the brain responds to burning ketone bodies. However, those predisposed to mental health issues such as anxiety and depression may feel these effects more acutely, meaning the ketogenic diet might not be their best choice.

4. Going Keto Restrict Your Fruit and Starchy Vegetable consumption.

Entering ketosis demands you to restrict particular consumption of fruit and vegetables, which can make it hard to consume enough vitamins, minerals, and fiber to be healthy. Many high-carb whole foods are treated very healthily, so if you are not careful to keep your nutrient levels in check, following the diet for the long term could lead to health problems.

5. Easy to Accidentally Eats Unhealthy Fats.

The Ketogenic diet set up fats above all other macronutrients, but beginners may have difficulty in knowing which ones to devote in. Many individuals who make an attempt to go Ketogenic fail to choose value fats like those that originate from plants and organic or grass-fed animal production. Filling up on canola oil or other "low" fats can be hurtful for your health in the long run.

6. Potentially hazardous to eating disorders at risk.

As with some other diets, the ketogenic diet requires scrutiny of every meal you eat, which may pose a danger for those with a history of disordered eating. It can become obsessive for some people following the eating plan, and categorizing so many foods as "off-limits" can lead to negative associations with food that are physically and mentally damaging. Similarly, failing to follow the diet perfectly could lead to feelings of guilt and inadequacy, all of which should be carefully weighed before starting.

7. Might Trigger Kidney Stones.

When they switch to a kidney diet, some people inflict damage to their kidneys because they consume too much meat and don't drink enough water. This may lead to an increase in uric acid, known to cause stones in the kidneys.

"If you're going to do keto, there's an excelling and worse way to do it." Loading meat on your plate, and particularly processed meats, can increase your risk of kidney stones and gout. High intake of animal protein makes your urine more acidic and raises levels of calcium and uric acid. This combination makes you more exposed to kidney stones, while high uric acid can increase your risk of gout. "Of course, a responsible keto diet plan need not result in kidney damage. A 2007 study on the development of a keto diet among young participants found that taking oral potassium citrate tablets appeared to be effective in monitoring meat consumption.

8. Potential for Ketoacidosis.

If you get too long into ketosis, you risk developing excessively high levels of acids in your blood, leading to a condition called ketoacidosis. This can leave you queasy, breathless, and mentally confused. It could lead to hospitalization in extreme cases.

9. Might Cause Digestive Distress.

The high-fat low-carb diet has the promising to lead to digestive problems, such as diarrhea or constipation, when you first transition to keto eating. Typically the symptoms disappear after a few weeks, but at first, they may be alarming.

Bad Breath is Common

One transient and inconvenient side effect of ketosis entry is breath "fruity." This is because your body breaks down acetoacetic acid, which many people say gives nail polish a similar odor. Your urine often smells the same way while in Ketosis.

Ketosis could affect your Athletic skills

The evidence is mixed about how athletic performance is affected by the ketogenic diet, and some people find this eating strategy hurts their outcomes. Athletes looking to maximize their power may struggle with a low carbohydrate diet to put on weight and improve their strength. Still, endurance athletes who need to sustain their energy for long periods might become more efficient if they fuel themselves in fat stores. Even so, it's harder for athletes to follow the diet than less active people because of the difficulty of powering yourself without carbs properly.

You may get the "Keto Flu" When the body acclimatizes to the ketogenic diet, and you may be going through a change period that leaves you feeling tired and exhausted. Eating plan followers call this the keto flu, and it can make you feel weak, light-headed, irritable, mentally slow, constipated, and lethargic. The symptoms tend to die down in a few days to a couple of weeks.

Dos and Don'ts of the Keto Diet *

If you're ready to try following the ketogenic diet, then from day one, you have to set up yourself to be successful. Below are a few dos, and you should not bear in mind when you first start.

Dos:

- Hold on healthy fats, such as eggs, avocado, and extra virgin olive oil.
- Eat low-carb greens to maximize your nutrient intake as much as possible.
- Eat real food made from whole (not processed) ingredients;
- Source as much as possible of organic, grass-fed animal products;
- Stay hydrated-helps offset fiber loss in your diet.
- Hold a food diary to keep track of how you feel over time.
- If the restrictions are too severe, consider a modified keto diet;
- If you have underlying medical conditions, check with your doctor before starting.
- Consider nutritional coaching to ensure the correct follow-up of your eating plan.
- Replace the electrolytes with bone broth.

Don'ts:

- Avoid consuming fast food as much as possible (even in keto-friendly meals, the fat content is low quality).
- Before you eat, don't avoid looking at nutritional information-most foods that have more carbs than you would expect.
- Avoid the use of "bad fats," such as corn, soya, canola, or hydrogenated oil.
- Avoid any processed food listed as low-fat, since most manufacturers compensate for lack of extra sugar (carbs) flavor.
- Don't over-consume. The high satiety of keto-friendly food could mean that at mealtimes, your place looks emptier than it did before. Avoid getting overwhelmed by habit.
- Don't strain on calories. There's little need to track the amounts if there is where your macronutrient ratios should be.

- Avoid consuming too many nuts or dairy products, as they are typically dense in calories and easy to over-eat.

Chapter 5

Mistakes in Keto Diet

The ketogenic diet, or Keto, is a low-carb eating approach embraced by many trying to lose weight and improve health. The carbs are typically reduced to less than 40 grams per day after a keto diet. This has been shown to outcome in weight loss, and may also improve heart health and control of blood sugar. Nonetheless, this must be done properly to reap the benefits of the keto diet.

Let's check things that might sabotage your efforts to lose weight on a keto diet.

1. You eat Too Many Carbs.

One of the main reasons people on the ketogenic diet don't lose weight is because they consume too many carbs. Carbohydrate intake must be drastically reduced to reach the ketosis state— a metabolic state in which your body scorch fat for energy instead of glucose. Only about 5 percent of your total calories will come from carbs. This contrasts sharply with the standard dietary recommendation that 45–65 percent of calories should come from carbs.

It's normal when you first adjust to the ketogenic diet, to have some difficulty cutting out carbs. Carbs must, however, be reduced to the recommended range to reach and maintain Ketosis. To minimize weight on a ketogenic diet, carbs have to be reduced to reach the ketosis state and induce the burning of fat.

2. You are not eating nutritious foods.

The crucial to a healthy weight loss is to consume nutritious, whole foods, no matter what dietary plan follows. Even if they are keto-friendly, relying on processed foods can put a dent into your weight loss. Adding between meals in foods such as snack bars, keto desserts, and other packaged foods can derail your weight loss work with the extra calories that they provide. Additionally, consuming too many convenience-type foods like hot dogs and fast food can slow weight loss when you're on the run. These foods are deficient in nutrients, which means they are high in calories but low in vitamins, minerals, and antioxidants.

Stick to unprocessed whole foods to maximize your nutrient intake when losing weight on the keto diet. Full-fat dairy products, fish, eggs, pastured meats, poultry, and healthy fats such as avocado and olive oil are all great choices, for example.

Make sure to add to the dishes non-starchy vegetables such as onions, broccoli, peppers, and mushrooms to add nutrients and fiber. To optimize weight loss following a ketogenic diet, avoid eating too many processed foods, and focus on meals and snacks containing fresh, whole ingredients instead.

3. You may be consuming too many calories.

The creation of a calorie deficit is critical when trying to lose weight. This can be achieved either by minimizing the number of calories you consume or by expending more calories by increasing physical activity. If you change to a keto diet and are not watching your calorie intake, it is unlikely that you will drop pounds.

Because many keto-friendly foods are high in calories, including avocados, olive oil, full-fat dairy, and nuts, it's important not to overdo it. After eating ketogenic meals and snacks, most people feel more satisfied with the filling effects of fat and protein.

However, by eating large portions or snacking on high-calorie foods throughout the day, it is entirely possible to eat too many calories on a ketogenic diet. It can help to create the calorie deficit needed to lose weight by paying attention to portion size, adding physical activity, and snacking in moderation between meals.

It's important to create a calorie deficit when following any diet to promote weight loss. It can help you drop excess pounds by curbing portion sizes, limiting snacks between meals, and getting more active.

The ketogenic diet, along with other healthy lifestyle improvements, can be an effective tool for weight loss. There are, however, different reasons why some people might fail to see the outcome they desire.

Consuming too many calories, lack of activity, chronic stress, underlying medical conditions, and not meeting the prescribed amounts of macronutrients can all have an adverse effect on weight loss.

To maximize a ketogenic diet's weight loss, get adequate sleep, reduce stress, become more active, and consume whole, nutritious, low-carb foods whenever possible.

Common Keto Mistakes

The keto diet is super-contrary, so it can be tough to get it "right." You'll have to nix starchy veggies on this diet, limit fruits and avoid grains, sauces, juice, and sweets, for example. And, by the standard keto food list, you'll have to load (lots of it) onto fats. Doing so will kick you into Ketosis, the metabolic state that triggers your body to burn fat in place of carbs, potentially speeding up your weight loss.

Nonetheless, as carbs are in just about everything and fats, they come in various forms (not all healthy), making mistakes here can be easy, especially if you're a keto lifestyle novice.

To help make sure you follow this approach as safely as possible, avoid the following common keto pitfalls:

The common mistakes are:

1. Cutting Your Carbs and Increasing Your Fat Too Much Quickly

One day you eat cereals, sandwiches, and pasta, and the next day you decide to hop on Keto and consume only 20 grams (g) of carbohydrates a day, which is often the recommended amount to start with. (For reference, a medium apple has 25 g of carbs.) That could be a drastic change for your body. Consider easing yourself in. "Before starting a keto diet, people may benefit from reducing their intake of carbohydrates rather than reducing cold turkey carbs.

2. Not Drinking Sufficient Water on Keto.

Do not forget about what you are sipping for all the focus on what you are eating. Dehydration on Keto is a greater possibility. "The drastic reduction in the consumption of carbohydrates on a ketogenic diet will cause fluid and electrolyte balance changes. Carbs are stored in the body along with water, so that water is lost along with them as these stores become depleted. The body flushes out urine buildup of ketones, which also depletes the body's water and sodium. Drink up all that, to say. Wake up to a large glass of water and sip regularly all day long to reach the goal of consuming half your body weight in ounces of water every day.

3. Not Prepering Yourself for the Keto Flu.

During the first two weeks of a keto diet, when your body changes from a carbohydrate burner to a fat burner, you feel what is known as "keto flu," or flu-like symptoms (including muscle cramps, nausea, aches, and fatigue). (It doesn't happen to everyone, FYI.) If you're not prepared for that feeling, you might think something is drastically wrong and give up your diet altogether. Plus, you can help yourself through the low-energy transition period by planning your meals or preparing meals. She also recommends eating potassium, magnesium, and sodium-rich foods, as well as hydrating to help ease symptoms of keto flu.

4. Forget about eating foods that are high in Omega-3 fatty acids.

While fat reigns supreme in the diet, turn not only to bacon, cheese, and cream. When selecting your fats, aim to include more anti-inflammatory omega-3s, especially EPA and DHA, the type found in salmon, sardines, oysters, herring, and molds, Clevenger says. (If you don't have fish, you can also take cod liver oil or krill oil.) Some healthy fats are also a good choice; if you haven't stocked up on avocado, olive oil, and seeds like flaxseed and chia seeds, you're sure to. Not only are they Keto compliant— but they also deliver good polyunsaturated and monounsaturated fat that your body needs to function in the best way possible.

5. Not salting your food enough.

You're probably not used to auditioning the call to eat more salt with people eat more sodium than always in a diet rich in processed foods do. But it's necessary for Keto. Not only does ketone clearance cause the body to lose sodium, but you may get far less table salt (which consists of forty percent sodium and sixty percent chloride) now that you've kicked out the top fount of salt in the standard American diet: packaged, processed foods including bread, chips, crackers, and cookies. "If you follow a ketogenic diet, possibilities are you will need to prepare most, if not all, of your meals and snacks from scratch, so just season with salt.

6. Going it alone and not clearing the Diet with your Doc.

Many followers of the keto diet try this because they hope to use it for a medical condition therapeutically. If that's you, first speak with your doctor and make sure they're on board with your plan— especially if you're taking medication, too. "Your healthcare practitioner might need to adjust some medications as your signs and symptoms improve. Just one example is insulin, because now that you are severely limiting carbohydrates, a lower dose may be necessary.

7. Not Paying The Attention to Your Veggie Intake.

Vegetables come with carbohydrates. And that means you've got to watch how much you're eating-even lettuce. If you're not careful about it or eat it as a chaotic situation, you might over-consume carbs and get kicked out of Ketosis. On the other hand, if counting every baby carrot gets too complicated, you may be skipping veggies altogether. Yet getting in vegetables (these contain fiber that prevents constipation, a potential side effect of Keto) is crucial when keeping portions in mind and properly counting carbs. Go for non-starchy options for a variety of nutrients in a rainbow of colors, such as leafy greens, cucumber, broccoli, tomato, cauliflower, bell peppers, and asparagus.

8. Getting caught up in the carb-counting and forgetting the quality of that food.

When it seems as if the sole purpose of Keto is to cut carbs drastically, the rest can feel like an afterthought.

"Reducing your consumption of carbohydrate is nice, but focusing on foods of higher quality when budget allows will also help improve your health," says Clevenger. This means choosing omega-3-rich foods, such as wild salmon, grass-fed, local or organic meats, and snacking on whole foods instead of keto-approved treatments. It also means trying to pursue a balanced diet as best as you can by eating as many fruits and veggies rich in nutrients as possible. Many registered dietitians are not a fan of Keto, because it can lead to deficiencies in nutrients. When consulting with an RD yourself when you practice Keto, you can help avoid those.

9. You eat too saturated fat.

One of the common dietary mistakes people make about Keto is eating too much drenched and trans fats. Yes, the keto diet is a high-fat diet, but there is still a dissimilarity between the fat types you should consume. Healthy fats are the ones that should build up your fat intake to the full.

Limit the intake of saturated fat. Too much-saturated fat can increase your "bad" cholesterol, so your risk of heart disease and type 2 diabetes can increase. While eliminating saturated fat from your diet can not be complete, don't let it make up the majority of your diet.

On the other hand, healthy fats are the ones that elevate your "good" cholesterol, which are monounsaturated fat and polyunsaturated fats. So stock up on your intake of nuts, avocado, and fatty fish. Your body will be grateful for that. We've been trained to be scared of fat, but that doesn't have to be the case, particularly on the keto diet. The key again is to consume the right kinds of fats.

Some of the best fat origin you should be consuming on this diet include:

- Wild-caught salmon, according to doctors and nutritionists.
- Organic olives.
- The Lawyers.
- Muzzles.

- Olive petrol.
- Oil to MCT.
- Butter made from coconut.
- Tallow oil to grass-fed beef.
- Ghee.

The fats you should stay away from at all costs are:

- Vegetable and canola oils–they are high in omega-6 fats, oxidizing, and riding. Also, these oils contain trans fats, which increase your "bad" LDL cholesterol and increase your risk of coronary artery disease. Most processed foods include foods containing trans fats.
- Dairy–Inflammation, acne, allergies, and skin conditions such as eczema, congestion, asthma, sinusitis, IBS, constipation, and weight gain are thought to cause this group.

Dairy is only an appropriate item to consume when you're a calf.

Not surprisingly, there is disagreement within the medical and nutritional community over the fat-to-protein ratio that you should be consuming. Some of what you're going to read online calls for more fat than protein, but some of the most reputable sources say the opposite is true.

Some sources recommend that 60 to 80 percent of your calories come from fat, while others say you should allocate those percentages to protein instead. The way forward is to eat balanced, whole foods.

If you will consume most of your calories from fats and proteins, make sure they are unprocessed and "clean." By cleaning, we mean eating grass-fed meat and pasture-raised meat, avoiding dairy, and staying away from processed junk food.

It's also possible that individuals respond to these ratios differently, and you may need to experiment to see what works for you. How do you figure this out? By having your ketones tested.

10. Not Getting sufficient electrolytes.

That also falls into the micronutrient department, but because it is so important, it gets its section.

You might want to suggest an electrolyte replacement if you experience keto flu symptoms such as fatigue, muscle aches, and exhaustion, brain fog, and nausea.

Here's why: You the find yourself urinating more when you start the keto diet first, and your body is burning off stored glucose (aka, glycogen). That's because you're releasing stored water as you burn glycogen, too.

An increase in urination is temporary, but keeping your electrolyte levels is always a good idea, especially if you work out regularly.

How to fix it

Electrolytes includes the minerals:

- Sodium.
- Compound calcium.
- Potatoes.
- Magnesium.

Make sure you get enough of these through:

1. Adding a supplement to high-quality electrolytes.

2. Add more low-carb nutrient-dense foods to your day, including leafy veggies, grass-fed meats, nuts, and seeds.

3. Before your workout, add some high-quality sea salt to your morning water, or drink light salted water.

Let's check out some symptoms to know you're in Ketosis

Signs You're Moving into Ketosis

1. Keto breath.

If you get a fruity, acetone, or metallic smell to your breath, you get what's known as "keto breath." When your body turns to burn fat for energy instead of glucose, the byproduct is ketones, and when you start producing ketones for the first time, your body will create more of them than it would initially be using. Once your body has no other glucose stores to draw from for energy and begins to become more adept at using ketones for energy, typically keto breath resolves.

2. Weight loss.

Many people follow Keto for the benefits of weight-loss, which can be significant, especially if you stick to the lifestyle for a long time. But you may experience rapid weight loss when you start on the Keto first. This is because Ketosis has a diuretic impact on your body, resulting in a rapid loss of water weight (take steps to stay hydrated, for this reason). You'll experience more fat loss over time as your body becomes more used to Keto and converts fat into ketones for fuel.

3. Fatigue.

Fatigue is an ordinary and short-term side effect of transitioning to a ketosis lifestyle. Typically, this is because of dehydration. Your body produces less insulin when you cut back on your carb intake and uses up its glycogen stores. Your body sweats more water with the glycogen when that happens (which is why you tend to lose water weight quickly on Keto). The rapid weight loss of water can cause dehydration, making you feel more fatigued. This is another reason you want to keep yourself hydrated. It's also a reason to add a pinch of Himalayan salt to your water; it will help compose your electrolytes, which are likely to get depleted with the rapid loss of water.

4. Decreased energy for exercise.

When you start Keto first, fatigue can extend to exercising with the same amount of energy you're used to. You may feel that you just don't have it in you at all. That's fine. When you begin a keto diet, decreased performance is also normal and short-term. If your body is used to burn glucose to power your workouts, and glucose is vacant due to a lack of carb intake, your body will try to figure out where to find energy. Once your body adjusts to reach for ketones as its source of fuel, you're not only going to be back to your regular performance levels, and you might also find that you have even more stamina. Give yourself some weeks to adapt to Keto and dissipate the symptom.

5. Suppressing appetite.

Two specific hormones affect our hunger and appetite. One hormone is called the hunger hormone ghrelin. The other hormone is cholecystokinin (CCK), which makes you feel complete. There is a decline in these two hunger-related hormones with increased ketone levels, and you end up feeling less hungry and more satisfied between meals. You will also find that you can comfortably go without eating or feeling hungry for longer periods and will have fewer cravings for processed / sugary foods.

6. Cognitive Performance Improved.

You can experience some brain fog during your keto initiation, but after a few weeks, expect better cognitive performance all-around, why? It's because he likes ketones in the brain. Studies show that ketones enhance all cognitive functional areas, including mental clarity, attention, and concentration. You may also encounter improved mood and decreased symptoms associated with anxiety.

7. Digestion issues.

When you start on Keto for the first time, and your body is not used to digest large amounts of fat, you may initially notice certain digestive problems such as diarrhea or constipation. Taking digestive enzymes designed to help with fat digestion may be helpful during the transitional period. That may be helpful with diarrhea. Be sure to eat a clean keto diet with adequate vegetables for fiber for constipation. Like the other initial symptoms of transition to a keto diet, digestion should improve upon adjustment of your body.

8. Insomnia.

One indication you're adapting to the changes that come with Ketosis is the difficulty of remaining asleep. Studies show you may initially sleep on Keto in shorter stages of REM or "dream." Things should be resolved within a few weeks, though.

9. Muscle Cramps.

The body produces less insulin when you cut back to very low carb intake (insulin stores the glucose in carbs). With smaller insulin, your kidneys release more sodium, which may throw out of balancing your other essential electrolytes and cause temporary muscle cramping. As with fatigue, you can help balance your electrolytes and give you some relief by adding a small portion of Himalayan salt to your water.

10. Increased Ketones in the blood.

The easiest way to confirm being in Ketosis is by using a blood test meter to test your ketones. Once the ketone levels are at or above 0.5 mmol / L, you are in Ketosis. Once your body becomes fuel with ketones, your ketone levels may drop some from the initial rise. This is not to say you're not in Ketosis. So long, so the ketones register at or above 0.5 mmol / L, you're in Ketosis!

All the above signs are signals that you are in Ketosis and on your way to the next stage, and the ultimate goal of a ketogenic lifestyle: fat adaptation. It can take several weeks to several months to be "fat adjusted," or completely converted to rely on fat for energy. But once you're there, the benefits of continued fat loss, sustained energy and focus, less hunger and irritability between meals, and improved overall health will be reaped.

Chapter 6

General Nutritional Meal For Women Over 40

When you age, your body changes, and your diet often needs to change. You eat what you are eating, right? Eating the right foods involves even more important for women over 40 to avoid health problems. So as we get older, it's not just our wardrobe and music taste that is changing. Our metabolism starts to decline gradually after age 30, which means we need to be even more selective about the foods we eat. There is a smaller room for empty calories from sugary beverages, desserts, and snacks, and more demand for high nutrient-to-calorie foods. At the same time, many people cultivate a greater appreciation of healthy eating as they age, and are on the lookout for multitasking foods that can help lower blood pressure and cholesterol and protect against diseases such as type 2 diabetes.

Eating a variety of whole foods is the key to a healthy diet, but some foods— including those highlighted below— offer your buck more nutritional bang than others. Powerhouse ingredients such as beans and leafy greens provide much-needed vitamins and minerals and help the body stay fit metabolically, making them great daily staples for the 40 + crowd. That is not to say that the age limit for these foods is set. Those picks provide premium fuel to energize your body, whether you're 4 or 94.

There are no big surprises or trendy ingredients on this list, and that's deliberate. All these featured foods are relatively affordable and readily available, which means they are well within reach of their health benefits.

1. Beans.

Eating a daily portion of beans or lentils (3/4 cup) can help lower 5 percent LDL ("bad") cholesterol. People with type 2 diabetes discovered that eating about a cup of beans or lentils per day as part of a healthy diet minimized hemoglobin A1C, a blood sugar control marker, by 0.5 percent, which is a significant improvement. Need an easy way to incorporate more beans into your diet? For a quick weekend meal, toss canned, low-sodium beans with whole-grain pasta and sautéed veggies.

2. Oats.

In women over 55, the risk of heart disease increases dramatically, so incorporating more cholesterol-lowering foods such as oats into your diet is a smart move. Oats are abundant in the form of soluble fiber called beta-glucan, and it has been shown that eating at least 3 grams of this fiber per day (equivalent to 1.5 cups of cooked oatmeal) decreases total and LDL cholesterol levels by 5 to 10 percent. People who regularly eat oats and other whole grains also run a reduced risk of early death. For other healthy ingredients such as nuts, seeds, and fruit, plain oats are cheaper than boxed cereals and a perfect conduit.

3. Apples.

They are definitely not as glamorous as acai berries or mangosteen, but apples are as excellent as exotic fruits, and much, much cheaper. A large apple provides 5 grams of heart-healthy fiber, and a daily diet of apples can reduce both total and LDL cholesterol to help keep your ticker in tip-top form. A study conducted in 2013 found that frequent apple eaters present a lower risk for type 2 diabetes. Additionally, the good news is, apples can be found almost everywhere, including gas stations and convenience stores. Slice one up and add a peanut butter smear to a classic snack that will never get old.

4. Nuts.

Snacking on nuts in place of chips, crackers, and cookies is an easy way to deliver a major upgrade to your diet. Eating one ounce of mixed nuts per day as part of a Mediterranean diet can reduce the danger of heart disease, heart attack, and stroke death by 28 percent. Furthermore, don't forget that peanuts also count, and they're just as healthy, but cost about half as much as almonds and other tree nuts. Another easy way to get into a daily service: use brown rice and quinoa as a garnish for roasted vegetables or whole-grain sides.

5. Leafy Greens.

Piling at meals on the spinach, kale, collards, or other leafy greens can help keep your mind sharp as you age. People who consume one to two servings a day had the same ability to cognize as people 11 years younger who barely ate greens. Cooking greens needn't be complicated. Take a baby spinach bag for a hassle-free side dish and sauté the leaves whole in an olive oil drizzle with optional chopped garlic. Heads up: If you are taking Coumadin's blood thinner, you don't have to give up entirely on greens; talk to your doctor about changing your prescription to allow for small portions every day.

6. Berries.

You want to get your berries filled too, another potential brain booster. Strawberries, blueberries, and their sister fruits are rich in phytochemicals that can help slow down age-related memory by enlarging blood flow to the brain and reducing damaging inflammation. These findings are still preliminary, but given their high fiber and vitamin content, berries are a healthy choice regardless of future research results. Fresh berries aren't always an affordable option, but at supermarkets, you can find big 2-to 3-pound bags of frozen varieties at an affordable price year-round. To give your diet a berry boost, add a scoop to plain yogurt, oatmeal, homemade muffins, or even the occasional ice cream bowl.

7. Yogurt

Eating adequate protein spread throughout the day can help preserve your muscle and slow down the gradual decrease in lean body mass that occurs as our bodies mature. Yogurt, especially Greek varieties, at breakfast and snack time, can provide a generous dose of high-quality protein, the times of the day when we tend to eat carbide meals. Cow's milk yogurt and fortified non-dairy versions are also good sources of calcium, a nutrient that women over the age of fifty and men over the age of seventy required to maintain bone health in greater quantities. However, the beneficial bacteria that give its tang to yogurt may also help to nourish the gut. Buy the plain stuff and doctor it with healthy mix-ins such as fresh or dried fruit, nuts, seeds, whole grain cereals, or (for a treat) dark chocolate chips to keep added sugar to a minimum.

Diet changes women over fifty should make right now.

1. Calcium for healthy bones.

Osteoporosis receives quite a lot of attention, and older women realize that with age, the risk of developing this bone disease rises. 1 in 3 women over 40 is at risk of osteoporosis, causing bone breakage.

"We absorb less calcium as we age, and some women's ability to tolerate milk— the best sources of calcium— also decreases as they get older." Other good sources are dark leafy greens and calcium-fortified orange juice." Women over 40 require 1,200 milligrams of calcium daily. To keep track of your consumption, use the Nutrition Facts mark on food products.

2. Protein for healthy muscle mass.

Older women are more likely to sit and exercise less. That compounds a process of natural aging called sarcopenia, which is the loss of muscle mass. Women may have lost as much as half of their skeletal muscle mass by the time women reach 80 years. Eating enough protein reduces the muscle wasting's effect.

"Healthy plant-based diets that don't involve meat, a major protein source, can still provide plenty of protein if you make savvy choices." Choose more soy, quinoa, eggs, dairy, nuts, seeds, and beans.

The protein that you need depends on how much you weigh. Experts approve 1 to 1.5 grams of protein per kilogram of weight for women over 40, (1 kilogram= 2.2 pounds). For example, if you scale 160 pounds, you would need a minimum of 63 grams of protein a day.

3. Vitamin B-12 for brain function.

In aging, women consume fewer nutrients from their food. Vitamin B-12, which is essential to maintaining both healthy red blood cells and brain function, is a key nutrient they may not absorb enough of.

"The best cause of vitamin B-12 are eggs, lean meats, milk, fish, and fortified foods such as cereals and grains." "Vegetables, in particular, will need to choose more covered foods, but even elderly people who eat all foods may have difficulty enthralling enough vitamin B-12." While the urged daily intake of vitamin B-12 for women over fifty is 2.4 micrograms per day.

Three tips for helping women over 40 obtain the nutrition they require.

- Consider whole food as a foundation for your diet. "Focusing on fruits, whole grains, and veggies will help prevent a lot of common age-related problems."

- Drink before you are thirsty. As you age, the way your body senses thirst changes. "Be sure to drink plenty of water, even if you don't feel thirsty. Carry a bottle of water and drink every meal with a glass."

- Make an appointment for food. You can create concrete plans which outline exactly how you are going to get key nutrients. "Write the plan to a calendar, simply by making an apple' appointment;' you're more likely to eat it."

4. Cinnamon and turmeric.

Another thing to go is taste, as we get older. "Aging causes a decline in the production of saliva and the ability to perceive taste, which means you may want to start experimenting with different spices, including turmeric." Turmeric has been shown to improve immune function and also decrease joint inflammation and prevent arthritis in older women. Other research has shown turmeric, and its main active ingredient curcumin may have a real effect on the prevention of Alzheimer's disease and some cancer forms.

Cinnamon is another spice to add to your cooking mix. "Cinnamon is well-known as an anti-inflammatory and anti-microbial agent. Cinnamon also helps maintain blood sugar control because it slows the rate at which the stomach empties after meals, resulting in high and low blood sugar." Studies also suggest a therapeutic use of cinnamon for type 2 diabetes, as it appears to improve the body's insulin sensitivity. "In people with kind two diabetes, it has been proved to have as little as one gram of cinnamon daily to reduce blood sugar, triglycerides, LDL (bad) cholesterol, and total cholesterol."

5. Broccoli and other leafy greens.

Protecting your eyes is key as time goes on, especially as a lot of eye issues come with aging. Lutein, which is connected to beta-carotene and vitamin A, is a valuable nutrient for optimizing your vision and preventing macular degeneration. And most of those over 40 are not getting enough of it. Green leafy vegetables are excellent sources of Lutein along with grapes, oranges, and egg yolks.

Check out these general healthy eating guidelines aside from adding the foods we mentioned to your diet:

- Decreasing saturated fats is valuable to prevent cardiovascular disease, so focus on healthy fats derived from nuts, lean meats, fish, low-fat dairy, olive oil, and plant-based sources such as avocados.

- Given that metabolism slows with aging, it's important to adjust how many calories you eat every day. Even if you are active, you still have to do this. The range is usually 1,400-2,400 calories per day, with men having a greater calorie count.

- Remove or minimize refined, processed foods, and beverages such as cookies, chips, sweets, cakes, and pastries. These processed foods contribute to increased body-wide inflammation, which then increases the risk of cancer, diabetes, and heart disease.

- Consider additives and multivitamins. "Supplements are generally important for seniors, but you need to discuss what you are taking with your doctor.' Apart from supplements, a gender-and age-specific multivitamin is also important.' More on that. As you age, you mislay muscle mass, about 10 percent every decade after age 45.' While you lose muscle, you are more likely to gain body fat and require fewer calories.'

More on this

You lose muscle mass as you age, about 10 percent every decade after 45 years of age. "While you lose muscle, you are more likely to get body fat and require fewer calories," she adds, "because the muscle burns more calories than the body fat.

Prioritizing exercise is also essential — especially resistance training to help counteract that decline in metabolism that happens with aging.

Nutrition must be given priority to prevent heart disease, diabetes, and other conditions that are of more significant concern as people grow older.

Eat fatty fish.

Shutterstock.

"Every week, having at least two 3.5-ounce portions of cooked fatty fish such as salmon, tuna, or herring can help to keep your heart healthy strong. These fish provide omega-3 fatty acids that help the heart. They are essential for the overall health of a person and are promoted for their protective effects, particularly on the brain, heart, and eyes.

Eat prunes.

Bone health matters as you age. Around one-third of women and 20 percent of men over the age of 40, due to osteoporosis, will break one bone. "Eating prunes helps reinforce bone health and keep your bones healthy." She adds that eating five to six prunes a day has been shown to help prevent bone loss, according to a study at Osteoporosis International. "You can snack prunes, add them to a salad, or make jams or even brownies with them."

Eat tomato sauce

Surprisingly this Food is helping to avoid wrinkles. "Tomatoes are red gems that equip the antioxidant lycopene." She adds that this antioxidant can help protect the skin from wrinkles and other damage caused by UV light. Cooked tomatoes are preferred because the lycopene is best absorbed by your body. You can add tomato sauce to the pasta, or use it in a recipe for spaghetti squash.

Limit added sugars.

All people should limit the intake of added sugar, and as you get older, this is even more important. "Added sugar such as brown sugar and table sugar should make up no more than 10 percent of your total calories." That's about 12 teaspoons of added sugar for a 2,000-calorie daily diet. "I recommend using one which offers some nutrition for the added sugar that you add to your day. My favorite is pure maple syrup.

"It's a unique sweetener because it features 60-plus health-helping polyphenols as well as mineral manganese blood-sugar-helping and B vitamin riboflavin, she adds. "I like using it to sweeten grains overnight, a muffin recipe, or a maple-Dijon salad dressing."

Take a multivitamin daily.

It will fill in any gaps in your image of nutrition. But make sure it's tailor-made for your age group. You need less iron when you're over 40 than younger women.

Some times a week, enjoy a vegetarian meal.

Plant-based diets have a great many benefits. They are smaller in calories but rich in minerals, vitamins, and antioxidants.

Cut down on salt.

Too much salt is linked to hypertension. The 2015 Dietary Guidelines, recently published, once again warn everyone to restrict salt to 2,300 milligrams a day.

Curb down the sweets.

Limit sugary beverages and desserts, and dairy sweetened products. They have little nutrition and can be loaded with calories.

Chapter 7

Gentle Approach To Keto For Women Over 40

Keto explodes. No longer only has the province of cutting-edge bodybuilders or enthusiasts of Longevity and warriors of neurodegenerative diseases, Keto invaded all walks of life. In the grocery stores, coffee shops, spin classes, business meetings, dinner parties, morning talk shows, I learn about that. Women make up the biggest group of recent diet entries according to our blog and sales metrics. This is important, but it also comes with a small wrinkle: Just like fasting, when implementing a ketogenic diet, most women need to take special precautions.

A lot of women experience a slowing metabolism at a rate of around 40 calories per day at this age. Slowing metabolism coupled with less exercise, muscle degeneration, and the potential for heightened cravings can make weight gain control extremely difficult. There are plenty of diet options available to help weight loss, but the keto diet has been among the most popular recently. We have taken a lot of questions about the efficacy of Keto and how to adhere healthily to the diet.

The quality makes ketogenic diets so successful for weight loss, particularly in obese and seriously overweight diets. And that satiety which offers a psychological boost. Not just, you're not hungry. You don't get hungry because you're eating your body fat. You are eating fewer calories than you were because all the Food comes from inside the home. That's powerful, and it's perpetuating itself, leading to even greater weight loss and making Keto much more durable.

But this is a two-edged sword. Premenopausal women have more sensitivity to reduced calories than other variants in humans.

Such recommendations based on science will give you the answers you are looking for if you want to lose weight for women over 40 on Keto.

What is Keto?

Keto is a diet requiring the cutting of carbs and increasing fats to help the body burn more efficiently its fat stores. Ketogenic diets contribute to better health and weight loss. In particular, ketogenic diets have helped certain individuals shed unwanted body fat without intense cravings typical of other diets. Some people with type 2 diabetes have also been found to be able to use Keto as a way to control their symptoms.

How Ketogenic Diets Function.

Ketones are the focal point of the ketogenic diet. When the body runs low on blood sugar, the body produces ketones, a fuel molecule, as an alternative energy source. Ketones are produced when you lower the carb intake and consume just the right amount of protein.

Your liver can transfer body fat into ketones when you eat keto-friendly foods, which are then used by your body as an energy source. When the body uses fat as a source of energy, you are in ketosis.

In some cases, this permits the body to dramatically increase its fat burning, which helps to reduce pockets of unwanted fat. This fat-burning method not only helps you lose weight, but it can also ward off cravings throughout the day and prevent energy crashes.

What foods are keto-approved?

While it's easy to say that the keto diet is high on fat and low on carbs, when you're in the grocery aisle, it always seems a bit more complicated.

Here's a list of women over 40 on keto foods.

What Foods to consume on keto.

- Flesh: search for unprocessed meat because it has less (or no) carbs added.
- Fish and seafood: avoid the carbs added to the breaded fish.
- Eggs: prepared no matter how much you like.
- Vegetables: those who grow above the earth.
- Dairy: opt for high-fat milk; low-fat options have often added sugar to it.
- Nuts: good source of fat, but do not over-eat.
- Berries: too mild.

What Food does NOT feed on Keto?
- Sugar: the key to cut.
- Fruit: a small fruit is all right, but too much adds sugar to your diet.

- Alcohol/beer: too many calories and sugars.
- Starches: white bread, potatoes, pasta, and rice.

Keto-Fying Your Favorite Foods.

Depending on what you enjoy, the no-nono list above may include eating some of your favorite foods. It's always a challenge to embrace the restrictions of a new diet. Food and recipes can become so personal to our families and us that they are difficult to break away from.

Fortunately, there are easy ways to make alternatives to your favorite foods, so they fit inside the Keto or at least stay inside a closed window. This means you can still have a galore of sandwiches, pasta dishes! Typically, to most benefit, select carbohydrates that have a low glycemic index.

- Bread: 20x fewer carbs than regular bread.
- Pasta: recycled2-ingredient.
- Rice: Recipe made with three ingredients.
- Oatmeal: Breakfast choice with low carb.

Is a Keto Diet Good for Women Over 40?

Whether Keto is good for you or not, depending on some factors that presume you are not suffering from health problems, a ketogenic diet can bring many benefits, especially for weight loss. Eating a great balance of greens, lean meat, and unprocessed carbs is the most important thing to remember.

Simply sticking to whole foods is probably the most effective way to eat healthily, mainly because it's a sustainable tactic. It's valuable to note that a lot of research shows ketogenic diets are hard to stick to. The best advice is to find a healthy way to eat that works for you, for that reason.

With that in mind, how can we refrain from the common pitfalls women face on Keto?

1. For the First Week, eat extra fat.
Or so this has three effects:

First, it regulates your fat-burning machinery construction. By boosting AMPK, it hastens your mitochondria's adaptation to the new fuel source.

Second, it helps to ensure that you don't work from a caloric deficit. This sends an abundance signal to your body, which means it won't dive into the mode of metabolic conservation and hang up for dear life on fat stores.

Third, that will give you a psychological boost. It's a nice way to realize you can eat more fat than you thought it would be useful and still lose weight and have health benefits. It also helps many of us break through the psychological barrier with eating fat, thanks to growing up in the era of "low-fat-everything." In the beginning, permitting yourself to eat a lot or perhaps even "too much" fat swings the pendulum fully in the other direction so that it can settle comfortably in the middle where it belongs.

Unless you're trying to gain weight, this huge increase in fat should not remain. You can start chipping away from your adipose tissue and reduce the amount of dietary fat as you get better at creating and burning ketones, and later body fat. However, continuing the extra fat intake may be important for those who are underweight or who therapeutically use Keto. However, this may be the case for any of us:

If you've been eating a low-fat diet so far, an apparent "big increase" in fat intake could just help you achieve what would be considered normal keto levels.

Make sure that you eat the particular fats that boost AMPK (which builds fat-burning mitochondria):

- Marine fat high in the long-chained EPA and DHA omega-3s.
- Polyphenol-rich extra virgin olive oil.
- Palmitoleic acid, a monounsaturated omega-7 fat. Everyday staple foods such as whale blubber, sea buckthorn berries, and anglerfish liver and mac nuts are the best sources.

2. Don't try to curb calories.

Recall how inadvertent calorie restriction is a big benefit in Keto? Do not try by further restricting them to double up.

Look. See. Give me three weeks if you don't buy these—three weeks of eating Ad-libitum. Don't wallow yourself. Don't just put a butter stick in your coffee because of that. Yet, don't count calories. Weigh not, and do not measure.

Eat it up to satiety. Eat until you have run out of hunger.

Don't eat until you burst. I am not talking about a fine line here. You've got a lot of wiggle room between "under-eating" and "gorging." A wide walkway is closer to that. Most people eat a whole basic diet. The primal keto diet will have no trouble staying in between the lines. Trust your subconscious systems will regulate your calorie intake. Do not attempt to override that system. Allow it to do work.

3. Fasting, or Keto: Select One.

Even many men, who tend to be impervious to metabolic insults, suffer from intense fasting or constantly compressed eating windows when combining extremely low carbohydrate diets. Its calories are getting too low, too fast, too long.

Keto is about boosting fat burning. Fasting is about boosting burning fat. They shoot for very similar things when you boil down to it. Combining the two seems like it would overcharge the advantages, and it can sometimes, but that's not always the case— especially for women, especially right before you start.

Furthermore, if you throw both in at once, it becomes difficult to disassemble the various inputs to decide what causes the harm (or benefit). Put in one major shift at a time— fasting or keto— and give yourself a clearer picture of the situation.

4. Avoid fat bombs that are poor in nutrients.

Fat bombs can be useful allies for hard-charging keto athletes who just need as many calories as possible to keep homeostasis going. Usually, these folks achieve adequate micro nutrition due to the sheer volume of food they eat, so there is "room" for coconut oil spoonful and olive oil shot glasses. If that is not describing you, do not do what they are doing.

If you are going to make a "fat bomb," make it as nutrient-dense as you can.

- Egg yolks, soft boiled eggs, salad with eggs (2-3 hard-boiled eggs cut with mustard and mayo).
- Avocados, avocados chopped with sardines and dressed topped with Green Goddess.
- Guacamole loaded with vegetables: avocados, salt, lime, chili peppers, herbs, tomatoes, garlic.
- Smoothies with Primal Fuel and Collagen Fuel.

Big Jelly Salad.

- Wrap the tuna in seaweed: make the tuna salad, wrap it with the nori sheets.
- Celery sticks with nut butter — add salt if not salted.
- Organic olives.

- Two ounces of cheese.
- Pork rinds (Why don't beef rinds ever exist? Big Rawhide hogging all the supply?).

5. Don't be that strict.

There's a compelling case for super-strictness. Sticking as close as possible to the Keto for the first 3 or 4 weeks does wonder of fat-adaptation. But you're good once you're in there. The machinery is built to burn fat. Your mitochondria are good at switching fat to glucose. The kid shocked you with eating a baked gluten-free cookie isn't going to ruin the whole keto trip. They're going to bounce back. You're going to be fine.

The aim we all got into this keto thing, after all, is to better our metabolic resilience. To be capable of going off the rails without a problem and finding our way back. Stay strict if you are trying to stave off epileptic seizures, increase the effectiveness of cancer drugs, treat dementia, or require high ketone readings for any other medical reason. If not, don't be as strict.

6. Best Advice is sometimes the worst.

If the diet "is not working," which means that the person usually does not lose weight, there are three things you hear:

1. Bottom carbs up to 20 g.

2. To a lot of protein.

3. To a lot of calories.

Yet less is not necessarily the answer for a stressed body. Sometimes your body needs more food period, maybe even more specifically carbs or protein. That's why I flinch when I see people going aligned from the Standard American Diet, or fair from higher-carb paleo / primal or the like, right into hardcore keto plus IF and extreme calorie restriction all in one fell swoop. The body needs time to discover how to run itself on ketones so it can be extremely harmful to take away all the food security at the same time. And since women are inherently more sensitive to metabolic disturbances or "famine" signals than men, they especially need to heed that warning.

7. Beware of Slippery Slope with Low Protein.

The slippery slope, they say, is a fallacy. In some cases, perhaps, but I see one valid example: the slippery low-protein slope. A woman is going Keto, and it has poor results. She goes online, asks around, suggests others, "How much protein do you eat? "She drops protein, gets worse, drops a little bit more protein, and suffers more. Soon she only eats Primal Kitchen mayo, mac nuts, romaine lettuce, and a single egg. She is so ketotic she is peeing purple drink, yet her symptoms are gradually only getting worse.

Yes, protein is a donor of oxaloacetate, meaning too much of it may impair ketogenesis. Sure, people who require high levels of circulating ketone bodies for their wellbeing will restrict protein, often more than they think. Yes, conventional diets for epilepsy are very low in protein. But a protein intake is such that it is too low, especially for women who lean to eat fewer protein than men in the initial place. It's not worth much to get high ketone readings if you're losing muscle mass, lagging in the gym, and experiencing worse shifts in body composition. I mean, for what, anyway, are we doing Keto?

Finally, going to Keto can pay huge dividends, but it has to be done properly— and women have less room for mistakes. I hope today's post provides some helpful tips to make it work. That said, I'm also going to offer the assurance that there's no keto version that's perfect for everyone (or any woman)—the same with Primal or any other way to eat. Just because your neighbor drowns all in sour cream and eats 4000 kcal/day in a 4-hour eating window, and making it Keto doesn't mean you have to do that. Get comfortable with the fact that it will be a learning process to find a way to eat, which works for you. With this guidance above, streamline your keto lifestyle — and a healthy dose of patience.

Chapter 8

Keto Diet For Longevity

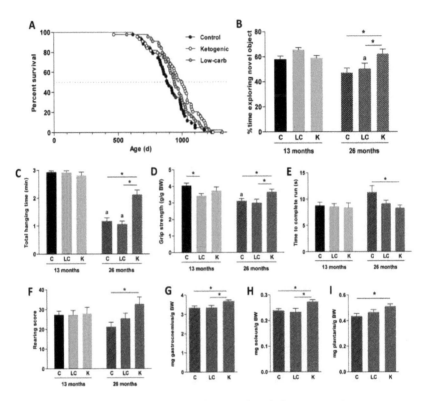

Low-Carbohydrate Diets Alter Physiology and Metabolism

We measured body weight (BW) and arrangement, a panel of serum biomarkers, energy expenditure, and physical activity to examine the physiological and metabolic changes caused by those diets. Despite being fed the same quantity of calories throughout the study, mice fed an LCD were heavier than mice fed either a control or KD. Analysis of body composition showed that lean mass in control and LCD mice increased with age and was significantly lower in KD mice at age 26. Compared to control or ketogenic mice, LCD mice had significantly more fat mass. Total fat mass peaked in all diet groups at age 17 months.

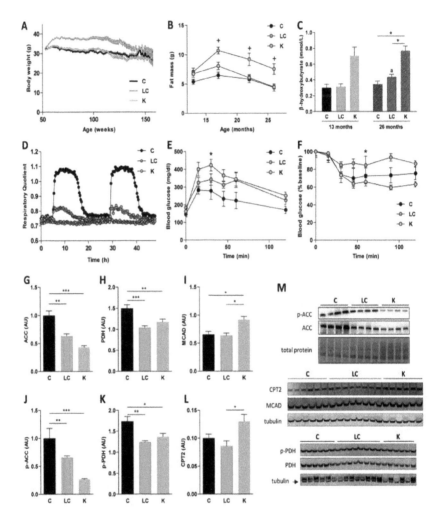

Male mice metabolic adaptations to low-carbohydrate diets.

(A) Body weights during a study of Longevity (n= 43–44).

(B) Fat size from 1 to 14 months of dietary intermediate (n= 15); += greater fat mass ($p < 0.05$) for the LCD compared to the other groups.

(C) β-hydroxybutyrate levels in circulation, 3 hours postprandially.

Animals were on the diets for one month for the physiological tests (D–F) and the protein levels in the liver (G–K). (D) RER for each dietary group during two 24 hour cycles (n= 7). (E) GTT at a speed of 16 hours, the area below the curve (AUC) differs between the KD and the control (n=6). (F) AUC differs between the LCD and the KD after a 4-hour fast (n= 6).

Quantification by Western blot of levels of (G) ACC, (H) PDH, (I) MCAD, (J) p-ACC, (K) p-PDH, and (L) CPT2 protein in the liver. (M) Each protein displays representative blots. For each case, representative load control is displayed (n= 4–8).

Diets: C= control, LC= low hydrocarbon content, K= ketogenic.

zwischen diets $p < 0.05$.

A$p < 0.05$ 13-mo to 26-mo for the same diet.

Following this common diet about weight loss, life expectancy could increase. Diet plays a big part in the life expectancy of a person, with certain foods increasing disease risk and others promoting good health. Which diet is considered best for Longevity boosting, though?

One can achieve a long life expectancy by eating the right foods. Eating at least five rations of a variety of fruits and vegetables each day and drinking plenty of fluids partly six to eight glasses a day is vital to fulfilling these feet.

It is also important to base meals on higher fiber starchy foods such as potatoes, bread, rice or pasta, possess some dairy or dairy alternatives, eat some protein, and choose unsaturated oils and spreads. But when it comes to following an overall diet-one that has been shown to improve the life expectancy of a person-which one is considered best? Studies have found a diet low in carbohydrates will increase the lifespan of a person.

So if you've been struggling to find a longevity diet that you can enjoy while at the same time increasing your Longevity and youthful appearance, you'll find the answer for Longevity with this Keto.

Ketosis is a metabolic model in which most of the body's supply of energy comes from the ketone bodies in the blood, as opposed to a glycolysis state in which blood glucose provides energy. Generally speaking, ketosis occurs when the body metabolizes high-rate fat and converts fatty acids into ketones, where you burn ketones instead of glucose for fuel.

The Ketogenic Diet merely reverts to the diet of good healthy fats and protein in our ancestors, while significantly reducing refined sugars and other carbohydrates!

Studies have shown that restricting carbohydrates on its own can increase your lifespan by 20 percent! Furthermore, it is particularly important to note that too much protein is responsible for an unwanted insulin/glucose response. So while on the Ketogenic diet, you should have no more than about 6 ounces of meat per meal.

No doubt, improving our cognition and protecting us from neurodegenerative diseases will help us live better. But can the ketogenic diet help us to live longer, too? In other words, is the diet capable of increasing both health duration and lifespan?

Research suggests that could be.

Researchers fed either a ketogenic or carbohydrate-based control diet to mice in the UC Davis study. Almost everyone involved had been surprised by the results.

Mice lived longer on the ketogenic diet— their median lifespan was 14 percent higher than the control— and lived better. The ketogenic diet slowed down cognitive decline and retained the engine function as they agreed. If these results were translated into humans, that would amount to an additional 7 to 10 years of life.

So how exactly has the ketogenic diet boosted Longevity? Scientists don't even know.

Current theories include enhanced mitochondrial (energy) capacity, a more neuroprotective energy pathway, and appetite suppression, which could cause the same caloric-restriction effect shown to increase the lifespan in dozens of animals and loosely associated with the longer lifespan shown in most of the world's popular Blue Zone populations.

However, our strongest clue comes from an ancient signaling path named mTOR. Stimulate mTOR and tell the body to grow, inhibit it, and tell it to repair. So if you want Longevity, you need to inhibit mTOR, and the most effective way to do this is by moderating protein, limiting carbs, and fueling predominantly with fat, which are the key features of the ketogenic diet.

It seems a little overzealous to suggest cutting carbs can help you live longer, but there is quite a bit of analysis showing that the keto diet can:

- Reduce inflammation associated with aging.
- Promoting gut microbiome.
- Encourage a healthy control of body weight (and metabolic biomarkers).
- Improve cognitive function.

A recent murine study, for example, has shown that feeding keto diet mice increased their lifespan and physical strength. Instead of focusing on weight loss, this study was primarily conducted to identify the metabolic adaptation in response to a keto diet and how it affects our body as we age.

The mice were divided into three groups during the study:

- Group 1-Mice were fed a regular high-carb rodent diet.
- Group 2-Low-carb / high-fat diet was given to mice.
- Group 3–Mice have eaten a ketogenic diet (85-90 percent of total fat caloric intake).

The study revealed:

1. The mice's lifespan in group 3 (fed the keto diet) was significantly increased compared with groups 1 and 2.

2. Group 3 experienced an increase in the function of memory and motor, including coordination and strength.

3. The keto diet enhanced the increase of inflammation markers associated with age.

4. The incidence of malignant tumors decreased.

Over some time, both humans and mice appear to follow similar patterns of metabolic change in response to a keto diet.

Chapter 9

Exercise For Women Over 40 In Support Of Keto

Being on a low-carb diet does not mean exercise is totally out of bounds. In fact, exercise can still reduce your risk of heart disease, obesity, and other health conditions. It's great for mental health, too.

Exercise is a perfect complement to a keto diet. Learn the right way to exercise to improve weight loss, develop muscle mass, and keep energy levels high.

Going keto means a significant reduction in carbs. Since these macronutrients are the body's primary source of fuel, you may be wondering about your best exercise options for ketoing.

The good news is that exercise is one of the most important decisions you can make for a healthy diet and overall health. To help you explore the advantages of a keto diet and to eliminate misconceptions, research with keto can provide great health benefits.

The types of exercise you prefer have to be careful. Talk with your physician or a certified personal trainer— and / or nutritionist — to make sure you select the best workouts to support your narrow-carb diet.

During certain exercises the diatribe may also affect your performance, and you can not work as intensively or as often as you are used to. You can not still use exercise to maintain the health of your heart, manage your stress and improve your overall health. This is not enough.

An outstanding place to start is to learn how to pick fruit, vegetables and meat. Be aware of the quality of foods that you eat in a keto diet–and keep the state of ketosis steady–is your first step.

Training is not only one of the key pillars of good health, but also plays a vital role in your ketogenic way of life. It can help improve cardiovascular health, increase the slender body mass, boost your bones and incredibly good your psychological condition.

Luckily, it is feasible and even beneficial to carry on keto, above all when trying to prevent signs of "keto flu." You just have to remember the following simple things.

Type of Exercise

Nutritional needs vary according to the type of exercise done. Training styles are generally divided into four different kinds: aerobic, anaerobic, flexible and stable.

Aerobic exercise, also known as cardio exercise, is anything more than 30 minutes in duration. Low-intensity, steady-state cardio workouts can lead to increased burning of fat, making it a great option for those whose main objective is weight loss.

Anaerobic exercise is characterized by shorter energy bursts, such as strength training, CrossFit, or high intensity interval (HIIT) training. Carbs are the primary fuel for anaerobic exercise, therefore fat alone may not provide sufficient energy for this type of workout.

Flexibility exercises can stretch your muscles, support your joints and improve the range of motion in your muscles. Yoga and simple after-work stretches can increase your flexibility to avoid injuries caused by shortening your muscles over time.

Exercises on stability involve balancing exercises and core training. They can help improve your alignment, strengthen your muscles and promote better movement control.

Carbs, Exercise, and Keto

When you're working out on keto, the intensity is vital:

The body uses fat as its primary energy source during low-to moderate-intensity workouts (aerobic exercise).

Carbohydrates are typically the principal source of energy during high-intensity exercises (anaerobic exercise).

When you are in ketosis, you use body fat as your primary source of energy. This can make your keto journey starting with high-intensity exercise a little more challenging. As such, it could affect your physical performance with some side effects.

However, for those making anaerobic exercise the core of their activity plan there is a solution. It is known as the targeted ketogenic diet.

Targeted Ketogenic Diet and Athletic Performance

If you like to exercise higher intensity (sprinting or weightlifting) and enjoy exercising more than three days a week, you may want to consider changing your keto diet to suit your carb needs. In your case, adherence to the traditional ketogenic diet is unlikely to be enough.

The best and most reliable way to determine the optimum consumption of carbohydrate to help your lifestyle and health goals is to use a ketogenic calculator.

A keto calculator will help you figure out your macronutrients, support your weight loss journey, and give you an accurate value of how many carbs you can eat.

How to Use a Targeted Ketogenic Diet for Exercise

While on the standard keto diet (SKD) you would stick to 20-40 grams of net carbs per day, on the target ketogenic diet (TKD) these net carbs would have to be taken 30 minutes to 1 hour before high-intensity activity.

A good rule of thumb is to eat 15-30 grams of fast-acting carbs, such as fruit, 30 minutes before and 30 minutes after your workout. This will guarantee that your muscles have the right amount of glycogen to work both during exercise and during rehabilitation.

Sticking to this timeline allows for the precise use of carbs to eliminate any chances of ketosis. In addition, the regular keto diet ratios can be preserved throughout the remainder of the day.

If a person prefers low or medium aerobics, flexibility and stability, it should be well suited to a normal diet plan. Again, it is important to use a keto macro calculator to ensure that you select the right dietary version for your health objectives.

Health Benefits of Exercising in Ketosis

Ketosis may seem to impede the long-term performance of exercise, although it has shown significant advantages.

In a recent study, 2 to 3 times more burnt fat has been seen in average 20 months compared to high-carb athletes in a three-hour period, who eat low-carb for the average of 20 months. The low carb group in the same study used and replanted as the high carbon group the same amount of muscle glycogen.

Admission to ketosis could help maintain blood glucose during exercise in people suffering from obesity. Another study in Australia showed.

Therefore, ketosis has shown that athletes heal after a high-intensity training and avoid exhaustion during long periods of aerobic exercise.

Working Out on Keto: A Healthy Combination

It is also important to know fully, which Keto diet version is best to follow, when you start following a low carb, high fat diet and passion for high-intensity exercise.

Because of his famous carb-heavy philosophies, ketosis could have bad exercise rep. In fact, however, it has an ordinary, low-and moderate-level healthy place, and can easily be adapted to the lifestyles of those who are more active.

It is important that you have the best possible information about adopting a keto lifestyle and how you can reap the wonderful benefits it can provide for your health.

It is not a one-size-fits-all model that the beauty of a ketogenic diet is. And find out what works best for you, it simply takes a little tweaking.

Keto is one of the most common and sustainable diets with this adaptability. In combination with your favorite training, it leads to a healthy, long-term lifestyle.

Best workouts for weight loss

The best training for Keto does not automatically improve the loss of weight or reduce fat as quickly as you like. This is because other workouts do not always suit well with a restrictive diet like this, although living on the keto diet is healthy and feasible.

Most health experts recommend that people following the keto diet perform:

Low-intensity cardio workouts such as cycling, jogging, rec sports, or swimming

Strength training exercises such as weight lifting (fewer reps with lighter weights).

In general, they don't recommend training sessions that rely heavily on energy. Avoiding enough carbs will prevent your body from using energy stores that are easily accessible. Therefore, you should try to avoid:

Circuit training

HIIT workouts

Any workout you've never done before

Whatever you need to exercise short bursts of energy is not part of your exercise scheme if you follow keto. When you're on this diet, you shouldn't start a brand new workout. It is difficult enough to adapt to daily keto when it's used already for exercise on your body. Try not to implement at once too many new, severe changes.

Before you exercise on the keto diet …

Before you start working out after the keto diet, you should know a few important things. Do not practice this diet until the following factors are taken into account.

You need to make sure you're eating enough. Not only enough calories, but healthy fat enough. Exercise often uses carbs first, fat then when energy is burned during a training exercise. You won't be able to even have a simple exercise if you don't get enough nutrition. You might even put yourself at risk.

Avoid high-intensity workouts. More isn't always better— especially if you follow an extreme diet like keto. These workouts rely on carbs you've stored away, which you won't have if you follow a keto diet. Stick with low-intensity workouts, particularly during the first few weeks of your new diet.

Listen to your body. If your body is trying to convince you that it can't handle it, you shouldn't keep pushing yourself. Continuing symptoms of nausea, dizziness, or weakness are not common, and could indicate that your body doesn't react well to a low-carb diet that includes exercise.

The keto diet puts a lot of tension on your body and can take weeks to adapt to — if you change at all (this plan is not for everyone). Don't push yourself too hard for "fast" weight loss.

If you pace yourself, eat well, and pay attention to how you feel physically, you can lose weight on your keto diet. At the beginning, anyway.

So if you're a woman over 40 and you're trying to get rid of those unwelcome extra pounds? On the other hand, are you tired of feeling lethargic and tired all day and looking for proven, natural ways to look years younger and feel more energetic?

If yes, then the Ketogenic Diet might be the answer you're looking for.

It's hard to lose weight after 40. This is because our metabolism has slowed considerably. Through Keto After 40, you can find the best opportunity for older women looking to take care of their wellbeing and stay fit for life.

Keto is about 10% of the calories coming from carbs, 20% from protein, and the rest from fat. Carb intakes vary from person to person.

Keto Diet Concerns

Proper hydration and mineral balance–this is a clear concern for anyone, an athlete with high heat and humidity.

Side effects of a Keto diet

Side effects of Keto's diet may include constipation, nausea, and frequent urination, weight loss is almost instantaneous because you will lose water if you don't eat carbs: for every 1-part carb you eat, you store around 3-parts of water. You through to lose the water as soon as you restrict carbs.

Why a Keto diet (also called metabolically efficient)

When you train the body to change (gradually) to fat burning at higher levels of intensity, typical digestive problems and the need for fuel during exercise will be minimized. Your body likes carbohydrates or glycogen stored in your carbohydrate muscles through exercise. That said, moving can be painful and sluggish, but it can be accomplished. You use fat at low levels of activity. Right now, at rest, you're burning almost 100 per cent of fuel fat. The more you run, the more likely the body uses glycogen first.

Why Small Frequent Meals are Not Your Best Friend

If we feed the body properly, there is no reason to burn fat. These 5-6 small meals a day? If you want to lose fat, they're going to get in the way. There is no indication that those mini meals–or grazing and snacking–consume more fat. There is plenty of evidence that shows that frequent eating increases fat storage and stops fat burning.

How many more people stop at fast food restaurants when the drive-through is installed? They didn't want to take time or make an effort to get in, but as soon as it was easy to get through or deliver fast food sales tripled. It's the same thing for your body.

If you exercise progressively increases the greatest change is to your pre-and post-exercise needs. Over the next 24 hours of significantly hard or long workouts, an increase in protein can help repair muscles.

These are my recommendations for exercise and nutrition for women who eat a balanced diet but want to lose fat or optimize their lean: shorter, low-level endurance exercise–hiking, kayaking, cross-country skiing–less to eat, with a focus on protein and fat.

Examples:

Nuts and seeds

A simple shake of almond milk and protein

Before high-intensity exercise–a small amount of fat / protein carbohydrate will help fuel a strong start and continued energy for exercise at higher intensities more comfortably. During high-intensity exercise over two hours, plan to refuel every 60-to-90 minutes. If you're training for a race, practice what you're going to do on the day of the race during your training.

Examples:

Banana with nut butter

Tortilla, hearty rice cakes, or sweet potatoes with nut butter

Lara bar (*If you're in your kitchen: eat real food)

Triathlon and hiking don't have the same kind of fuel needs. You're going to be exercising at much higher overall intensity to complete a triathlon. Fuel appropriately.

Put Back in What a Keto Diet and Lifestyle Take Out

The more restrictive the diet, the more micronutrients are restricted by food alone. A well-formulated nutrient routine may be necessary to prevent long-term exhaustion, adrenal fatigue, or disease.

Exercise depletes micronutrients:

A, B, C E, iron, magnesium, manganese, potassium, selenium, zinc, alpha-lipoic acid, CoQ10

+

A Keto diet depletes micronutrients: B vitamins, calcium, and magnesium +

Stress depletes micronutrients: A, B vitamins, calcium, selenium, zinc, iron, magnesium, omega 3 and a few others

This is just a partial list of micronutrients depleted to illustrate the common denominators.

Frequent high-level or long-term preparation, which raise cortisols. Low level for 75 minutes or high intensity 45-60 minutes, start to increase cortisol in a negative way. Overall stress management is essential for a mid-life or an older woman to prepare for endurance events.

Signs of fatigue are typical to an endurance event. It's tricky to balance the progression of training, rest & recovery, and listen to your body. As a coach, I always want someone who is under-trained vs. over-trained. Rest when in doubt. Fatiga could be a lack of nutrients or a hormonal imbalance.

Goals, Micronutrients, and Meals

The goals are to reduce inflammation and time management so that she has a lot of energy during the preparation and the race day. She wants to recover easily from every exercise, so she's primed for the next one. Long-term, she'd like to focus on maintaining healthy muscle and bone density.

On the basis of an earlier evaluation, Catherine might want to decide how to boost the following micronutrients:

Multivitamin taken in multiple doses

Vitamin B, D, C, calcium, magnesium, Omega 3

After Exercise Nutrition

Post-exercise feeding for older adults should be 60 to 120 minutes. Catherine's increased frequency and intensity of training her post-exercise smoothie or high protein meal may come sooner.

It needs 20-35 grams of protein to prevent muscle loss, moderate carbs and fat from replenishing, and antioxidants and antioxidants to reduce inflammation. Research shows that older adults can benefit from exercise compared to younger subjects if they have almost double the protein (40gm compared to 20 g).

My favorite recovery smoothie is packed with all the above. Each ingredient has anti-inflammatory properties.

Post Exercise Recovery Smoothie

2 cups spinach

½ avocado

¾ cup frozen cherries

Paleo or Plant Power chocolate protein

Cacao powder (or nibs)

Unsweetened coconut milk

Check your fatigue level regularly. If training leaves you wanting to rest and recover the rest of the day or sleep changes so you don't want to get up or can't sleep: these are signs of overtraining in someone who normally sleeps well and wakes up. Get all of my own (and Flipping 40 Group preference) smoothie recipes PLUS the guide to special superfood additions.

Muscles in Minutes

Above all, whether you are exercising or training for an event that you want to avoid adrenal fatigue. Adrenal fatigue is a concern if you pursue a training program so rigidly. Listen to your body's need for more rest between sessions, or reduce the volume and increase the intensity of specific workouts.

Training for endurance events in a traditional way–with significant volume–as an older adult, along with nutritional changes–is a lot of change, potentially a lot of stress on your body at once.

Make sure you keep up with some strength training for both injury prevention and bone loss due to increased running and swimming. They are both great for muscles and health, but they eliminate the bone benefits of weight-bearing activity.

Best Rest

Track how well you're recovering. This will inform you how well your diet meets your needs. Slow signs of recovery include persistent soreness, or exhaustion, or decreased workout ability without growing complexity.

Take a simple heart rate every morning while you're still lying in bed. Track what occurs during lengthy workout days, rest days, and mild days. A heart rate that is 5 beats faster than the average for more than a couple days means that you need to get back out of training and have a major rest week.

You can also monitor **heart rate variability,** in other words, measure between heartbeats.

Assuming you have a 60 bpm resting heart rate. You may think the time between beats is a second, but it's not. In fact, the more variability you have between the beats of your heart, the better. It might be.8, 1.2 seconds, and so on. The more predictable your heart rate variability, the more you will do your best on a day of recovery instead of a day of training.

A special monitor and app is required. They're both taken first thing in the morning. Start with the heart rate of rest.

Another simple option is to track your sleep number, or your sleep IQ, just like my sleep number bed. I use a wearable device. Resting heart rate, heart rate variability, and your Sleep IQ help you focus on both rest and training. The first move is reacting to exhaustion, but if it's regular and chronic, it's a good idea to start looking for a better compromise between rest and exercise.

The Best Fats On Keto

Not all fats are equivalent. In reality, many of the fats used in supermarkets, fast food chains and processed foods on the food market produce unhealthy fats that can do more harm than good to your wellbeing.

There's more to a ketogenic diet than just eating fat. You will know what type of fat is better for keto and which fats to stop.

Approximately 70% of your calories come from food on a high-fat keto diet. If you're just starting a low-carb, healthy lifestyle, you might be wondering which fats are best for your health, and which are best avoided. To further clear things up, this article should explain the distinctions between good fats and bad fats.

You'll learn about the different kinds of fats and keto-friendly food sources for each of you. In fact, you can hear about where the theory of "fat is evil" started, and how it has since been debunked by research.

Good Fats on Keto

What are Good Fats to Eat on Keto?

Healthy fat sources to eat keto include saturated fats, monounsaturated fats (MUFAs) and some polyunsaturated fats (PUFAs). Sticking to foods that contain the fats mentioned above is the best way to approach your ketogenic diet when you create a low-carb, high-fat meal plan.

Monounsaturated fats have been shown to boost insulin sensitivity, raising the risk of heart disease and lower blood pressure.

Polyunsaturated fats should be used with a little more caution. Many PUFAs, such as Omega-3 fatty acids, are important to the safety of the brain and should be part of any healthy diet. However, when PUFAs, such as vegetable oils, are heated or oxidized, they may form harmful compounds, such as free radicals, which have been shown to increase inflammation in the body. This means that you should never use PUFAs for cooking, and these fats should always be eaten cold and never eaten if they are rancid.

Fats that get green light when it comes to keto diet — and good health in general — can be broken down into four categories: saturated fats, monounsaturated fats (MUFAs), polyunsaturated fats (PUFAs) and naturally occurring trans fats.

The reality is that all healthy fats contain a combination of these four fat forms. Nevertheless, the fat that is most prevalent (or can be contained in the largest traces) within the food source defines how the product is classified.

Healthy Keto Saturated Fats

Saturated fats have been seen as harmful to heart health for years and years. It led to a low-fat and fat-free craze around the 1970s, which is still being promoted by the American Heart Association. However, even this organization is slowly coming up with the idea that fat intake is part of a heart-healthy diet (although it continues to demonize saturated fats).

Recent studies also dismissed AHA's assertion that there is no clear correlation between saturated fats— which humans have been consuming for thousands of years — and the risk of heart disease.

In fact, in the case of good fats vs. bad fats, there are many benefits of including healthy saturated fats in your diet, including balanced hormones, improved cognition and better nutrient absorption.

Another form of saturated fat is medium chain triglycerides (MCTs), most of which are contained in coconut oil and in small amounts in butter and palm oil. The body can absorb these fats very quickly and, when consumed, they are passed directly to the liver for immediate energy usage.

MCT oil has some amazing health benefits, including better digestive wellbeing, appetite reduction (with possible weight loss), strengthened memory, enhanced immune system, decreased risk of heart disease, and improved athletic performance.

Good sources of saturated fat included in the keto meal plan include red meat, butter, ghee, heavy cream, lard, coconut oil, bacon, palm oil (trying to buy a better brand) and cocoa butter. When purchasing animal fats such as meat, eggs and dairy products, you always choose the highest quality that you can reasonably afford, including grass-fed meat and dairy and pasture-raised eggs.

Saturated fats includes

Butter and ghee **(clarified butter)**

Cream, whipping cream and coconut cream

Coconut oil

Cheese

Lard and tallow

Health benefits of saturated fats on keto can include:

Improved levels of HDL and LDL cholesterol, including increased HDL (good cholesterol) to prevent the build-up of LDL (bad cholesterol) in the arteries.

Maintenance of bone density

Boosting of immune system health

Support in creation of important hormones like cortisol and testosterone

Healthy Keto Monounsaturated Fats

In comparison to saturated fat, monounsaturated fatty acids (MUFAs) have been recognized as safe for many years. Several studies have linked these to the health benefits of good cholesterol and improved insulin resistance.

MUFAs can be found in many foods that are considered healthy and are a common pillar of Mediterranean diet. MUFA contains extra virgin olive oil, coconut and almond butter, macadamia nut oil, goose fat, cashews, pecans, lard and bacon fat.

Monounsaturated fats

Olives and olive oil

Avocados and avocado oil

Macadamias and macadamia oil

Almonds, Brazil nuts, hazelnuts, pecans

Lard and tallow

Health benefits of MUFAs on ketosis can include:

Increased HDL blood cholesterol levels

Lowered blood pressure

Lowered risk for heart disease

Reduced belly fat

Reduced insulin resistance

Healthy Keto Polyunsaturated Fats

Here's the main thing you need to remember about consuming polyunsaturated fatty acids (PUFAs) on a ketogenic diet: how you consume them counts. Once cooked, polyunsaturated fats can become free radicals that are unhealthy compounds that increase inflammation along with the risk of cancer and cardiovascular disease in the body. Therefore, many PUFAs should be consumed cold (for example, in salad dressings) and not used for cooking, and should always be stored at cool or room temperatures.

You will use PUFAs in the context of very refined oils as well as in very stable forms. The right types can provide a great deal of advantages as part of a keto diet, as they include both omega-3 and omega-6 fatty acids, which are essential nutrients. The sum of each is significant, however.

Ideally, the omega-6 to omega-3 fatty acid ratio should be about 1:1. Most Western diets eat a ratio of about 1:30, so focus on your omega-3 PUFA intake.

Healthy sources of PUFA include extra virgin olive oil, linseed and linseed oil, walnuts, fatty fish (like salmon) and fish oil, sardines, mackerel, sesame oil, chia seeds, nuts and nut butter and avocado oil. Those products, such as maize oil and canola oil, should be prevented.

Polyunsaturated fats

Omega-3

Fatty fish (salmon, mackerel, herring, sardines, anchovies)

Grass-fed animals

Dairy from grass-fed animals

Eggs from pastured chickens

Algae

Chia seeds

Flaxseeds

Hemp seeds

Walnuts

Omega-6

Found in almost every food, including meat, nuts and seeds.

Vegetable and seed oils **(especially safflower oil, sunflower oil, soybean oil, cotton seed oil and corn oil)** – as well as processed foods that contain them – are often a major source of omega-6 PUFAs in modern Western diets.

We recommend minimizing these vegetable and seed oils because they are highly processed.

Aim for a healthy omega-6: omega-3 PUFA ratio

Omega-6 PUFA linoleic acid and omega-3 PUFA alpha-linolenic acid are considered essential fatty acids because your body can not produce them on its own so they must be ingested in food. Alpha-linolenic acid is mainly found in plants.

Nevertheless, the most significant omega-3 fats are EPA and DHA, present in fatty fish and grass-fed meat. Such long-chain fats are essential to brain health, inflammatory regulation, and cellular function.

These may also may risk factors for heart disease, although the outcomes of high quality trials are mixed. Although alpha-linolenic acid can be converted into EPA and DHA in your body, conversion is not very efficient.

Achieving a balance of omega-3 and omega-6 fatty acids might also be important.

Our evolutionary diet is thought to include approximately equal levels of omega-3 and omega-6 fats. Nevertheless, as a result of heavy reliance on processed foods, many Western diets today can consume more than 15 times as much omega-6 as omega-3.

Since it's not obvious at this point how this dietary change could have an effect on our wellbeing, we feel it makes sense to stick with the food our ancestors have eaten for thousands of years. Eating fatty fish at least twice a week, selecting meat and dairy products from grass-fed livestock and consuming fewer processed food will help improve the omega-6:omega-3 ratio.

The healthiest fats to cook with

Saturated fats such as butter, ghee, coconut oil and lard are the best means of cooking and deep frying. Both fats are heat-resistant and do not oxidize at high temperatures, as do the less robust polyunsaturated fats in vegetable and seed oils.

Some monounsaturated fats, such as olive oil, are also good choices for high-heat cooking because they remain quite stable when heated.

It may be best to avoid using polyunsaturated fats–such as safflower or corn oil–when cooking at very high temperatures. When heated, these fats are more likely to be oxidized or damaged. Avocado oil, rich in monounsaturated fat, is also easily oxidized when exposed to high temperatures.

At this time, evidence suggests that vegetable oils are likely to be fine for shorter-heat cooking.

Nonetheless, in order to minimize the harm, we suggest that you cook with butter, lard or other heat-stable fats and use avocado oil to make salad dressing, mayonnaise or other condiments that do not involve heating.

Health benefits of PUFAs can include:

Decreased risk of heart disease and stroke

Decreased risk of autoimmune disorders and other inflammatory diseases

Improved mental health, reducing symptoms caused by depression or ADHD

Natural Trans Fats

When it comes to good fats vs. bad fats, you might be surprised to see trans fats in the "nice" fat group. While most trans fats are very unsafe and hazardous, certain products, such as grass-fed meats and dairy fats, naturally contain a form of trans fat known as vaccenic acid. The fat form can be found in animal products and dairy products such as grass-fed butter and yogurt.

Health benefits of vaccenic acid can include:

Reduced risk of heart disease

Reduced risk of diabetes and obesity

Possible protection against cancer risk

How are fats absorbed in the body?

Once fatty foods have been digested, their triglycerides are broken down into individual fatty acids and glycerols.

Both saturated and unsaturated long chain fatty acids are absorbed into the bloodstream, packaged with cholesterol and proteins, and transported throughout your system to be used or stored as body fat.

Long chain and medium chain fatty acids are processed differently. Instead of being transported throughout your body, it goes directly to the liver, where it can be converted to ketones and used as a quick source of energy.

 Additionally, they may be less likely to be stored as fat compared with long-chain fatty acids.

What is cholesterol?

Cholesterol is a waxy substance found in animal products only. It doesn't provide strength, unlike fatty acids. Nevertheless, the body needs it to generate steroid hormones, vitamin D and bile acids that help digest food.

All your cells produce cholesterol; in addition, most of the cholesterol in your blood comes from your tissue rather than the food you eat. Dietary cholesterol typically does not increase blood cholesterol levels significantly, if at all, and therefore is unlikely to increase the risk of heart disease.

How much fat should I eat?

Many individuals do not need to count calories or fat grams on a low-carb or keto diet. While keeping carbs low and protein in a wide, moderate range, most people can eat as much fat as they need to feel satisfied after a meal. This often makes it possible for body weight to remain within or to approach the desired range.

If you still want to calculate fat grams, follow these general guidelines:

The amount of fat you should eat on a keto or low-carb diet depends on a number of things, including your protein and carbohydrate intake, your current weight, and your weight goals. Were you trying to lose, hold, or gain weight?

Next, work out your protein and starch requirements, and then satisfy the leftover energy needs with fat. Generally, keto diets are heavier in calories than low-carbon diets. A keto diet usually contains about 70-80 percent of calories in fat, opposed to about 40-65 percent for a more moderate low-carb diet.

You might have learned that the more fat you eat on a keto diet, the more weight you lose. It's just not true. When you consume more food than you need to be full, it can slow down or stop weight loss, even if you have very few carbohydrates.

This also applies to medium chain fats found in coconut oil and MCT oil, which are normally burned rather than stored. Your body is less likely to burn its own fat if you have extra dietary fat coming in, regardless of the type.

Importantly, although adding less fat to food can help you burn more fat in your body, don't make the mistake of trying to follow a diet that's low in both carbs and fat — a strategy that will ultimately leave you hungry.

It's not healthy or sustainable to starve yourself long-term. Eat enough fat to feel full and satisfied after a meal, but not stuffed.

Once you're at your goal weight, adding a little more fat to your food while you're still eating the same amount of carbs and protein can help you maintain your weight for a long time. This usually happens automatically, if you follow the signals of your hunger.

Bad Fats on Keto

One of the great aspects of keto diet is the freedom to consume plenty of full and enjoyable dietary fats.

That said, it is important to learn about the types of fats that you may want to limit (or completely eliminate) your diet, as they may have adverse health effects.

Unhealthy, Processed Trans Fats and Polyunsaturated Fats

Processed trans fats are the types most people know about— and they can be very damaging to your health.

During food production, artificial trans fats are formed through the processing of polyunsaturated fats. That's why it's important to choose only PUFAs that are unprocessed, overheated, or otherwise altered. Not only does the PUFA process produce harmful free radicals, but trans fats are often produced from oils containing genetically modified seeds.

Examples of trans fats to avoid include hydrogenated and partially hydrogenated oils found in processed products such as cookies, crackers, margarine, French fries and fast food. They can also be found in processed vegetable oils such as cottonseed oil, sunflower oil, peanut oil, safflower oil, soya bean oil and canola oil.

Risks of consuming Trans fats include:

Increased risk of heart disease

Weight gain and increased body fat

Increased risk of cancer

Reduced HDL cholesterol and increased LDL, or bad cholesterol

Pro-inflammatory

Bad for the health of your gut

Chapter 10
Understanding The Different Types Of Fats

There are a few things we know for sure: fat is a big source of energy and supports healthy hormones. It is a mechanism for the synthesis of certain vitamins and minerals. Fat is also critical to the development of cell membranes, the important liner of each cell that promotes homeostasis and protects cells. For many body processes, we require fats.

Fat gets a bad rap, even though we don't need it in our food. Dietary fats are essential to boost your body's energy and cell growth. These even help to protect your lungs and help keep your body moist. Fat helps your body absorb nutrients and generate essential hormones, too. Your body definitely needs to be fat.

Do all fats have the same number of calories?

There are nine calories in every gram of fat, no matter what kind of fat it is. Fats are more energy-dense than carbohydrates and proteins, which provide 4 calories per gram.

Consuming high calorie rates–regardless of source–may lead to weight gain or overweight. High levels of saturated or trans fat may also lead to heart disease and stroke. Replacement of saturated fats and trans fats by monounsaturated fats and polyunsaturated fats–thus preserving a nutritionally adequate diet.

Can fats be part of a healthy diet?

Eating fat foods is definitely part of a healthy diet. Just remember to choose the food that gives you good fats and balance the amount of calories you eat from all foods with the amount of calories you burn. Purpose to follow a dietary routine that stresses the consumption of greens, fruits and whole grains; contains low-fat dairy products, poultry, seafood, legumes, non-tropical vegetable oils and nuts; and reduces the intake of salt, chocolate, sweetened sugar and red meat. It ensures that your food will be poor in both saturated fats and trans fats.

Types of Fat

Unsaturated fats

Unsaturated fats that are liquid at room temperature are called beneficial fats because they can boost blood cholesterol levels, relieve depression, regulate heart rhythms, and play a number of other beneficial roles. Unsaturated fats are primarily present in plant foods, such as vegetable oils, nuts and seeds.

There are two types of "good" unsaturated fats:

1. Monounsaturated fats, found in high concentrations in:

Olive, peanut, and canola oils

Avocados

Nuts such as almonds, hazelnuts, and pecans

Seeds such as pumpkin and sesame seeds

2. Polyunsaturated fats, found in high concentrations in

Sunflower, corn, soybean, and flaxseed oils

Walnuts

Flax seeds

Fish

Canola oil – though higher in monounsaturated fat, it's also a good source of polyunsaturated fat.

Omega-3 fats are an important type of polyunsaturated fat. The body can't make these, so they must come from food.

An excellent way to get omega-3 fats is by eating fish 2-3 times a week.

Good plant sources of omega-3 fats include flax seeds, walnuts, and canola or soybean oil.

Higher blood omega-3 fats are associated with a lower risk of premature death among older adults, according to the HSPH Faculty study.

Most people do not eat enough healthy unsaturated fats. 8-10% of calories per day should come from polyunsaturated fats, and there is evidence that eating more polyunsaturated fat— up to 15% of calories per day — instead of saturated fat can reduce the risk of heart disease.

Dutch researchers conducted an analysis of 60 studies examining the effects of carbohydrates and different fats on blood lipid levels. In studies in which polyunsaturated and monounsaturated fats were consumed in place of carbohydrates, these good fats decreased the levels of harmful LDL and increased HDL protection.

More recently, a randomized trial known as the Optimal Macronutrient Intake Trial for Heart Health showed that replacing a carbohydrate-rich diet with one rich in unsaturated fat, predominantly monounsaturated fat, lowers blood pressure, improves lipid levels and reduces the estimated cardiovascular risk.

Finding Foods with Healthy Fats is a useful visual guide to help you determine which fats are beneficial and which are harmful.

Saturated Fats

All products containing fat have a combination of different fat types. Some nutritious foods, such as chicken and nuts, contain significant levels of saturated fat, but often less than beef, cheese and ice cream. Saturated fat is present mostly in animal foods, although a few plant foods are also rich in saturated fats, such as coconut, banana oil, palm oil, and palm kernel oil.

The Dietary Guidelines for Americans require that fewer than 10% of calories be consumed everyday from saturated fat.

The American Heart Association went much further, proposing that saturated fat be reduced to no more than 7% of calories.

Cutting back on saturated fat is likely to have no benefit, however, if people replace saturated fat with refined carbohydrates. Eating processed carbs instead of saturated fat reduces "bad" LDL cholesterol, but often decreases "good" HDL cholesterol and raises triglycerides. The overall result is almost as harmful for the heart as consuming so much saturated fat.

The biggest sources of saturated fat in the diet are

Pizza and cheese

Whole and reduced fat milk, butter and dairy desserts

Meat products (sausage, bacon, beef, hamburgers)

Cookies and other grain-based desserts

A variety of mixed fast food dishes

Although decades of dietary advice suggested that saturated fat is harmful, this idea has begun to evolve in recent years. Several studies suggest that eating diets high in saturated fat does not increase the risk of heart disease, with one report analyzing the findings of 21 studies that followed 340,000 people for up to 23 years.

Researchers looked at the relationship between saturated fat intake and coronary heart disease (CHD), stroke, and cardiovascular disease (CVD). Their contradictory conclusion: "There is insufficient evidence from prospective epidemiological studies to suggest that dietary saturated fat is associated with an increased risk of CHD, stroke, or CVD."

A well-publicized 2014 report disputed the correlation between saturated fat and heart disease, but the HSPH nutrition experts considered the paper to be seriously misleading. To order to set the record straight, the Harvard School of Public Health assembled a group of nutrition experts to say, "Saturated or not: Does the form of fat matter?"

The overarching message is that cutting back on saturated fat can be good for health if people replace saturated fat with good fats, especially polyunsaturated fat. Eating good fats instead of saturated fat reduces "bad" LDL cholesterol and increases the ratio of total cholesterol to "good" HDL cholesterol which decreases the risk of heart disease.

Eating good fats instead of saturated fat can also help to prevent insulin resistance, a precursor to diabetes. Therefore, although saturated fat may not be as unsafe as once believed, evidence clearly shows that unsaturated fat is the healthiest type of fat.

Trans Fats

Trans fatty acids, more commonly known as trans fats, are produced by heating liquid vegetable oils in the presence of hydrogen gas and a catalyst, a process called hydrogenation.

Partially hydrogenating vegetable oils make them more robust and less likely to become rancid. The method often transforms the oil into a good, which helps it act as margarine or shortening.

Partially hydrogenated oils can withstand repeated heating without breaking down, making them ideal for frying fast food.

For these factors, partially hydrogenated oils have become the mainstay of restaurants and the food industry–despite burgers, baked goods and packaged snack foods and margarine.

Partially hydrogenated oil is not the only source of trans fat in our diet. Trans fats are also commonly found in small quantities of beef fat and dairy fat. Trans fats are the worst type of fat for the liver, the blood vessels, and the rest of the body because:

Raise bad LDL and lower good HDL

Create inflammation–immunity-related reactions– that have been associated with heart disease, stroke, diabetes, and other chronic conditions.

Contribute to insulin resistance

Can have adverse health effects even in small amounts–the likelihood of coronary heart disease rises by 23% for every extra 2% of calories from trans fat eaten everyday.

Chapter 11
OMEGA-3-6-9

Omega-6 fatty acids are fatty acids. Various forms are present in vegetable oils, including maize, evening primrose seed, safflower and soya oils. Some forms of omega-6 fatty acids are present in black currant seed, borage seed and evening primrose oil.

Omega-6 fatty acids are used under many conditions, but the best information that science can provide is that putting arachidonic acid, a particular omega-6 fatty acid, in infant formulas does not improve the development of infants. Adequate research has not been conducted on omega-6 fatty acids to determine whether they are useful for other applications.

Most of our knowledge on omega-6 fatty acid diets is derived from the analysis of common omega-6 fatty acids or vegetable oils containing omega-6 fatty acids. See the different lists of gamma-linolenic acid, as well as evening primrose, borage and black currant.

How does it work?

Omega-6 fatty acids are present all over the body. They're assisting with the work of all cells. When individuals do not consume sufficiently omega-6 fatty acids, the cells will not work properly. Too many omega-6 fatty acids can change the way cells behave and have harmful effects on the cells in the heart and blood vessels.

Uses & Effectiveness

Possibly Ineffective for

Multiple sclerosis (MS). Taking omega-6 fatty acids does not seem to prevent the progression of MS.

Infant development. Adding omega-6 fatty acid arachidonic acid along with omega-3 fatty acid named docosahexaenoic acid (DHA) to infant formula does not seem to boost the health, vision or growth of the brain of children.

Insufficient Evidence for

Attention deficit-hyperactivity disorder (ADHD). Taking omega-3 and omega-6 fatty acids twice daily for 3-6 months does not improve the symptoms of ADHD.

Heart disease. Different types of omega-6 fatty acids have a different effect on the heart and blood vessels. Some types appear to be protective in the body, while others may make the disease worse. However, omega-6 fatty acids, which are shown to be more harmful when found in higher amounts in the body, are not those typically eaten in the diet or found in supplements. Whether our body makes certain kinds of omega-6 fatty acids relies on other health and lifestyle influences.

A lung disease called COPD. Early research suggests that breathing problems are worse for people with COPD who eat large amounts of omega-6 fatty acids.

Developmental coordination disorder (DCD). Taking a mixture of omega-6 and omega-3 fatty acids for 3 months may improve reading, spelling and actions, but not balance or activity in children with DCD.

Diabetes. Those with more linoleic acid, a form of omega-6 fatty acid, are less likely to develop diabetes in their body than those with fewer.

Diarrhea in infants. Infant formula supplemented with omega-6 fatty acid called arachidonic acid and omega-3 fatty acid called docosahexaenoic acid (DHA) for the first year of life has a lower risk of diarrhea.

Respiratory illness in infants. Infant formula supplemented with omega-6 fatty acid called arachidonic acid and omega-3 fatty acid called docosahexaenoic acid (DHA) for the first year of life has a lower risk of lung problems.

Reducing the risk of heart disease.

Lowering bad cholesterol levels (LDL).

Increasing good cholesterol levels (HDL).

Reducing the risk of cancer.

Eyelid swelling.

To improve recovery after laser eye surgery.

Other conditions.

Omega-6 fats are found in:

Soybeans

Corn

Safflower and sunflower oils

Nuts and seeds

Meat poultry, fish and eggs

What are omega-3 fats?

Omega-3 fats are healthy fats that are unsaturated. It's crucial that we get them from the food we're eating. There are three forms of omega-3 fat:

ALA (alpha linoleic acid)

DHA (Docosahexanoic acid)

EPA (Eicosapentaenoic acid)

Omega-3 fats play a role in the development of the brain, nerve and eye in infants. These also help keep the immune system safe and can help reduce the risk of heart disease in adults.

Omega-3 fats are found in:

Fatty fish like salmon, mackerel, anchovies, sardines, arctic char and trout

Eggs (including omega-3 enriched)

Flaxseeds and flaxseed oil

Walnuts

Soybeans

Tofu

Canola oil

Fortified foods like some margarines, juices and yogurts

Omega-3 fats are a vital part of human cell membranes. We also have a variety of other key functions, including:

Improving heart health: Omega-3 fatty acids can increase the amount of "healthy" HDL cholesterol. These may also reduce triglycerides, blood pressure and the development of arterial plaques.

Supporting mental health: Omega-3s can minimize symptoms of depression, schizophrenia, and bipolar disorder. It can also reduce the risk of psychotic disorders for those at risk.

Reducing weight and waist size: Omega-3 fats play an important role in weight management and can help reduce the size of the waist.

Decreasing liver fat: Consuming omega-3s in your diet can help to reduce the amount of fat in your liver.

Supporting infant brain development: Omega-3s are particularly important for the development of the brain in children.

Fighting inflammation: Omega-3 fats are anti-inflammatory, which means that they can reduce the inflammation of your body that can lead to a variety of chronic diseases.

Preventing dementia: People who eat more seafood, which is rich in omega-3 oil, appear to have a smoother loss in brain function in old age. Omega-3s may also help to improve the memory of older people.

Promoting bone health: People with higher omega-3 intakes and blood levels tend to have better bone mineral density.

Preventing asthma: Omega-3 intake can help to reduce symptoms of asthma, especially in early life.

What Are Omega-9 Fatty Acids?

Omega-9 fatty acids are monounsaturated, which means that they have only one double bond. Nine carbons are found from the omega end of the fatty acid molecule.

Oleic acid is the most popular omega 9 fatty acid and the most abundant monounsaturated fatty acid in the diet.

Omega-9 fatty acids are not exclusively "necessary," which implies that they can be generated by the body.

In addition, omega-9 fats are the most abundant fat in most cells in the body. Nevertheless, eating foods high in omega-9 fatty acids instead of other forms of fat may have a variety of positive health effects.

One large study showed that high monounsaturated fat diets could decrease plasma triglycerides by 19 percent and "poor" very low-density lipoprotein (VLDL) cholesterol by 22 percent in patients with diabetes.

Another study found that feeding mice rich in monounsaturated fat increased insulin sensitivity and decreased inflammation.

The same study found that people who eat high monounsaturated fat diets had less inflammation and greater insulin sensitivity than those who consumed high saturated fat diets.

Foods High in Omega-9 Fats

Omega-9 fats are also common in vegetable and seed oils, nuts and seeds. There are no adequate intake recommendations for omega-9s, as they are non-essential.

Here are the amounts of omega-9s in 100 grams of the following foods:

Olive oil: 83 grams

Cashew nut oil: 73 grams

Almond oil: 70 grams

Avocado oil: 60 grams

Peanut oil: 47 grams

Almonds: 30 grams

Cashews: 24 grams

Walnuts: 9 grams

Should You Take an Omega-3-6-9 Supplement?

Combined omega-3-6-9 products typically have sufficient amounts of each of these fatty acids, such as 2:1:1 for omega-3:6:9.

These oils will help increase the consumption of omega-3 fats, which should be consumed more often in the Western diet.

As a matter of fact, such oils provide a good fatty acid composition so that the omega-6 to omega-3 ratio is less than 4:1.

Nevertheless, since most people already consume too many omega-6s and the body produces omega-9s, there is no general need to substitute such fats.

Therefore, it is best to focus the diet on a good balance of omega-3,-6 and-9 fatty acids. This should involve eating at least two servings of oily fish per week and using olive oil for cooking and dressing.

In turn, try to reduce the intake of omega-6 by reducing the use of other vegetable oils and fried foods cooked in processed vegetable oils.

If you do not have enough omega-3s in your food, it is best to take an omega-3 supplement on your own rather than a combined omega-3-6-9 supplement.

How to Choose an Omega 3-6-9 Supplement

Like other oils, polyunsaturated fatty acids can easily be oxidized when exposed to heat and light.

So, if you're buying an omega-3-6-9 supplement, choose one that's cold pressed. This means that the oil has been extracted with little pressure, reducing the degradation that can kill the molecules of fatty acids.

So make sure you are using a drug that is not oxidized, choose one that includes an antioxidant, such as vitamin E. In reality, choose a drink with the highest omega-3 content — ideally more than 0.3 grams per serving.

Therefore, because EPA and DHA have more health benefits than ALA, choose a supplement that uses fish oil or algae oil rather than linseed oil.

While combination omega-3-6-9 supplements have become very popular, they typically do not provide any additional benefit from taking omega-3 alone. Omega-6s are essential in certain quantities, but many of them are already consumed in many Western food items and men.

In fact, omega-9 fats can be created by the body and easily consumed in the diet, so you don't need to take them through the form of supplements. Thus, although the blend supplements contain perfect omega 3-6-9 amounts, drinking only omega-3s is likely to give you the most health benefits.

Chapter 12
Fat Bombs

Healthy fats are all raging-so much, heavy cream, butter, and oil packed into bite-sized portions is a nutritious snack.

So What Exactly Are Fat Bombs and Are They Actually Healthy?

While carbs may be the most easily accessible fuel to power your runs, fat plays an equally important role in driving miles. Once you've burned all the energy you've stored from carbs, your body turns to an almost unlimited amount of fat for more energy. Translation: In order to run faster, you need healthy fats.

For a number of years now, protein and sugar "bags" have been the preferred pick-me-up for the health-conscious. Fans of the little spheres-a tightly packed mixture of nuts, seeds and protein powders-say that they are perfect for wolfing down when energy levels are low.

Eat butter, not low-fat spreads.

Heavy cream, butter and oil are rolled into portions of the mash ready for a small boost in your mouth. It used to be anathema to healthy food audiences to suck a lump of fat–but once demonised fats were actually perfectly healthy. However, are these bombs the best way to consume good fats?

What are fat bombs?

They consist of a combination of ingredients like butter, coconut oil, nuts and seeds. Initially, fat bombs were built for Ketogenic followers. Devotees consume a highly fat, low carb diet, which induces ketosis, which starves the body, instead of carbohydrates, to be burnt with fat.

In the 1920s, Dr. Henry Rawle Geyelin introduced the epilepsy as a way to treat it. The diet became popular. Today the disorder is still recognized as an effective treatment, although its prevalence is probably better known among body-builders and dietitians.

We were trained to believe that fat is bad, but fat bombs can be healthy and effective, whether they form part of a high, low carbon diet or not. "Fat bombs could be a fantastic option for an in-house snack or snacks as it can help balance your frequently low or high blood sugar with a more carbonated diet."

But you must be careful in choosing fats that are safe for you. The largest amount of good fats are coconut oil, MCT oil, grease or ghee butter, coconut milk, heavy cream, avocado or avocado oils, sessamic or sesame seed oil, chia seeds, flax seeds and walnuts."

Avoid the' yellow oils,' known as industrial fats like canola, soy oil and vegetable oil, that are full of toxic byproducts and highly inflammatory and also remove the fat bombs from cheese that can be inflammatory and increase the desired LDL of cholesterol.'

Are Fat Bombs Healthy?

I know people have different opinions about how fat you can get in a day, so it depends, of course, on your own views and diets. Such therapies are not only rich in heart-healthy fat, but also completely free from refined carbohydrates and sugar, and fat tends to relax you with a small amount so it's not like cookies or candies that make you eat a tone and still hunger somehow.

Moderation is important for them as with anything, but it's so complete that even after only a small amount it's easier to feel fulfilled. It flies in the face of conventional nutritional wisdom that fat bombs are a good thing to eat. A high dose of fat is essential to enable your body to absorb other foodstuffs with the use of vitamins and nutrients, although this can be achieved in "very healthier ways: the upshot?

PART 2

Chapter 13
Keto Bread Homemade

This is the best low carb bread made from almond meal. Most recipes for keto bread can taste very eggy, or easily crumble. Surprisingly, there is little to no eggy flavor to this sandwich. Best of all, it holds together and works like wheat bread for sandwiches and toasties.

A combination of almond flour (or coconut flour), healthy fats, eggs, and xanthan gum is keto bread. It resembles normal textured wheat bread but has about 20 times fewer carbs than normal bread.

I Don't Have Xanthan Gum. What Can I Use Instead?

Xanthan gum is a binding agent stopping the bread from cracking, so it cuts like regular wheat bread. If you don't have xanthan gum, though, you have some options to replace it:

Gelatine Powder- Use 1 tablespoon.

Guar Gum- Use 1 cubicle.

Ground Chia seeds- Use 1 spoonful.

Psyllium Husk Powder- Use 1 spoonful.

Omit Xanthan Gum- The result is still good.

Ingredients.

6 Big eggs.
1/2 teaspoon cream of tartar.
¼ c. Butter (1/2 stick), melted, then frozen.
1 1/2 c. The almond flour is finely ground.
1 tablespoon bake flour.
1/2 cup cheap salt.

Guidelines.

Preheat the oven to 370 ° and line an 8"-x-4 "parchment paper loaf tray. Egg whites and egg yolks are separate.

Combine the egg whites and the tartar cream in a large bowl. Whip up until stiff peaks form using a hand mixer.

Beat yolks with melted butter, almond flour, baking powder, and salt in a small, large bowl using a hand mixer. Fold the whipped egg whites in 1/3 when fully incorporated, then fold into the remainder.

Pour batter over the loaf pan and top smooth. Bake for 30 minutes, or come out clean until the top is slightly golden and a toothpick inserted. Let it calm down for 30 minutes before chopping.

Nutrition (by serving): 440 calories, 19 g of protein, 10 g of carbohydrates, 5 g of fiber, 2 g of sugar, 40 g of fat, 11 g of saturated fat, 125 mg of sodium The keto bread contains two net carbs per bun (a similar regular bread bun may contain around 20 grams of carbs). This makes the ketogenic diet a decent option.

The ingredients and quantities used are important in all baking processes, and especially in low-carb baking. In this recycle the eggs and ground psyllium husk are difficult to replace.

If you don't like almond meal, or if you have an allergy, instead you can make this recipe with coconut meal. Replace the amount of almond flour as much as a third of coconut flour, and double the number of egg whites.

Sprinkle seeds on the buns before you put them into the oven for a different look and some snap-poppy seeds, sesame seeds, or why not some salt flakes and herbs?

Flavor your favorite seasoning with your bread to make it perfect for whatever you serve it with. You can use crushed caraway seeds, garlic powder, or seasoning your homemade bread.

As with all our low-carb and keto meals, the keto bread is 100% gluten-free.

If I Am susceptible To Almonds, Can I Use Coconut Flour Instead?

Add 1/2 cup of coconut flour instead of adding 2 cups of almond flour. The result will be very, very much alike, to using almond flour, despite the lower amount of coconut flour, as it is much more absorbable than almond flour.

How do I store Bread for Keto?

Normally I slice it up and put the bits in 2 plastic containers. Keep one container in the fridge for next week, and one container in the freezer.

How many carbohydrates are found in Keto bread?

This ketogenic recipe for bread has only 1 gram of net carbs. Full carbs are net carbohydrates, minus starch.

How many calories is in keto Bread?

Each slice of bread comes with 165 calories. This is better than regular bread, but only because there is a lot of healthy butter and coconut oil in it.

In the world of ketogenic bread, low carb bread is very popular, and most people are happy that there is keto alternative to regular bread. It also matches diabetics and the Atkins.

Chapter 14
Keto Pizza

There's plenty of great low-carb pizza options, with cheese, cauliflower, protein powder, almond flour, or even meat crusts. Homemade pizza can be a fun experience for the whole family; it's inexpensive, extremely flexible, and ideal for feeding a crowd. Anyone can turn into a professional pizza maker with a little preparation and practice, even if you've never created the pizza from scratch.

One of the most excellent things about homemade pizza is that all the ingredients can be handled! Choose the crust that best suits you, tailors the toppings to match your tastes–and don't skimp on the cheese. Many low carb pizza crusts made from fathead bread. This low-carb alternative to pizza is perfect if you are on a keto diet or just want to cut carbs, and is the vision of a carb lover with only three net carbs per slice!

Pizza is the heaven of carb, and one of my greatest weaknesses. Who can resist a cheese-laden, crispy pie? Now, with this super simple and delicious keto pizza recipe, you can have your slice and enjoy it too. The pizza gets together in no time with the time needed to get up. Before or after baking, it can be frozen, making it great for times when you want to order pizza. The dough is made with my "Fathead" version of the dough, which has been checked with different ratios and herbs.

Keto Fathead pizza dough ingredients
Mozzarella cheese
Cream cheese
Almond flour
Egg
Baking powder
Herbs

How to make keto fathead pizza
You'll use shredded mozzarella cheese, 1 oz (or two tablespoons) cream cheese to start with. Microwave

the cream cheese and mozzarella for 45 seconds, or until slightly melted. Then whisk until fully incorporated into the cream cheese. At first, it may seem a little tough, but it will soon be coming together.

The next step is to incorporate almond flour, baking powder, and herbs in the recipe. Mix until fully incorporated. The dough is going to look sticky, but that's fine.

You have to have options to roll the dough out: because the dough will be soft and gummy, you can either roll it between two sheets of parchment paper or wet or graze your hands and pat it flat with your hands.

The dough will have to be baked twice, once for baking the crust and the next for the cheese and toppings. It is baked for the first time in 10 minutes. While the first time it bakes, this would be a good time to make the toppings!

This is my preferred part, and where you can become very creative and make your pizza. Add your preferred sauces and toppings to the pizza crust and reappear to the oven to bake for another 6-9 minutes or until the perfect doneness is finished, and the cheese is melted and gooey!

Toppings.

We are increasing the pizza experience by adding these tasty low-carb ingredients to make pizza topping great.

Meat: pepperoni, ham, sausage, bacon, shredded chicken, ground beef, anchovies

Sauce: tomato paste, sour cream or crème fraîche, sun-dried tomato pesto, green pesto, salsa sauce

BBQ Chicken: While garlic sauce & BBQ sauce, shredded rotisserie chicken, red onion or caramelized onion, cheeses, and provolone mozzarella.

Buffalo chicken: Ranch or buffalo sauce, blue cheese dressing, shredded rotisserie chicken or grilled, caramelized onion, mozzarella cheese.

Pesto Chicken: house-made pesto sauce grilled or shredded rotisserie chicken and mozzarella.

Cheese: parmesan, mozzarella, goat cheese, blue cheese, feta cheese, shredded cheddar

Fresh or dried herbs: oregano, rosemary, basil, thyme

Veggies: olives, mushrooms, onions, artichokes, green bell peppers, cherry tomatoes, pickled jalapeños, broccoli

Southwestern style: Enchilada sauce shredded chicken cheddar and pepper jack cheese, black bean, onion, corn, and cilantro. Top with a creamy chipotle or cilantro sauce.

Chapter 15
Keto Recipes

Guilt-Free Smoothies That Taste Like Dessert

Always thought you could just have a brunch dessert? Well, now, with these guilt-free, healthy smoothies that taste like dessert–minus the calories–you can have your cake and drink it too.

They that drink like milkshakes but to start your day off right, these low-calorie dessert smoothies are filled with vitamins, calcium, and other energy-enhancing goodness. Plus, there's a cookie smoothie recipe from pumpkin pie to chocolate pudding to match any sweet tooth. Whether you're looking for a quick, easy, healthy breakfast or snack ideas, or need to sneak some nutrition into your children, dessert smoothie is a win for the whole family.

How to keep Dessert Smoothies from Becoming Calorie Bombs

Of course, you can blur the line between smoothies and milkshakes. But there are some easy ways to make sure that your dessert smoothie doesn't move into straight-up candy territory: use unsweetened cocoa powder instead of sugar chocolate syrup to fulfill your chocolate cravings without extra calories. Throw in some banana, avocado, and/or yogurt (to keep them healthy, make your dessert smoothies without ice cream— that's just a milkshake) for a rich, creamy texture that's packed with nutrients rather than empty calories!

To cut sugar, whip up the smoothie with naturally sweet strawberries, dates, or a little maple syrup or agave if you need a sweetness boost.

Recipes for the Desserty Smoothie.

Here are eight absolute favorite smoothie recipes that taste like dessert:

1. Pumpkin Pie smoothie.

Due to the pumpkin puree (an excellent source of vitamin A) and mild spices, this may taste like pumpkin pie, but it's as good as it gets to make it extra smooth with banana and yogurt. "I love making this smoothie. I sometimes add chia seeds for a bit of texture.' Add a splash of milk if the surface is too thick to your liking.'

2. Carrot Cake Smoothie.

With soy milk, mango, peach, carrot, and some bold spices, this is one of those rare flavourful vegan dessert smoothies that taste great and packs a nutritional punch.' This is one of those' outside-the-box' smoothies, and I li."

3. Superfood Cherry Smoothie Pudding.

If you're looking for more vegan fruit smoothies, don't miss out on this decadent taste, organic chocolate smoothie, made with the aid of banana and avocado. "A guilt-free way to please those chocolate cravings (which are constant in my case)," says the author of the recipe, Ergghlack. "I know the element may seem a little strange, but just like chocolate pudding, I swear these tastes!"

4. Paleo Apple Pie Smoothie.

This filling, paleo-friendly smoothie gets nourishment from apple, pineapple, cashew butter, and flaxseed meal." That smoothie is great when the calendar says it's autumn, but the outside temperature denies it. You can have a cool glass drop in! I used cinnamon spice instead of apple pie.

5. Strawberry Smoothie Shortcake

Including crushed shortbread cookies in the smoothie, this certainly teeters on the dessert edge. But it also has good-for-you milk, bananas, and complimentary protein powder to offer a healthy advantage to real dessert. "You can swap vanilla wafers with short-bread cookies if you want."

6. Chocolate Banana Smoothie.

Are you looking for more banana cake smoothies? This top-examined recipe gets high marks for being easy and delicious. Want to make it even healthier? "You can make this one with healthy ingredients, and it tastes just as good," recommends sticking a fork in

m. If you like, you can use some almond butter too. It turns out great this way, and it is healthful at the same time as long as there is no sugar besides the natural sugar in the banana. "

7. Pineapple Creamsicle Smoothie.

For slight sunshine in a glass, try this smoothie take on a nostalgic ice cream flavor. It's one of those dessert smoothies shakes the whole family will enjoy." This was delicious! A go-to recipe for my new smoothie. "This is perfect for an extra nutrient boost also with some new kale and ground flax." 8. Strawberry Nutella Banana Smoothie.

Is there anything that does not boost the distribution of chocolate-hazelnut? This certainly makes this chocolate smoothie with strawberry banana even more divine. "This is a quick and easy breakfast which even children love," Maggie T says. "With Greek yogurt, keeping you fresh until lunch is a decent amount of protein. Some blenders work best with strong materials next to the tip, and last added liquids."

Keto Lunch Ideas That You'll Want to Eat

1. Shrimp avocado salad, with feta and onions.

Summery seared shrimps with avocado, cilantro, tomatoes, and crumbled feta burst with flavor, and it takes only 15 minutes to make — make sure you cool the shrimp quickly before tossing the rest of the salad with it.

2. Bowl with Keto salmon poke.

Feel filled with this super fresh veggie-packed sushi bowl, and stay full. It is made of fresh salmon, shredded cabbage, cucumber, radishes, chunks of avocado, fresh herbs, and mayonnaise drizzle (keto) in sesame.

3. Chili Low Carb Keto.

This keto-friendly chili contains no beans. Instead, it's packed with beef fed with grass, spices, veggies, and tomato sauce. Top with cheese and sour cream just as you would like your favorite non-keto chili, and you're not going to feel like you're missing out in the least.

4. Vegetarian Wraps in Lettuce.

Lettuce wraps are a brilliant way to produce low-carb-if a dish usually high on carbs. Made with tofu, mushrooms, soy sauce, rice vinegar, sesame oil, hoisin sauce, water chestnuts, and spices, this filling is eaten on a bed of lettuce leaves.

5. Noodle Cucumber Salad.

This cold cucumber salad with tahini sauce, with some grilled chicken or seared tofu on top, would make a great lunch.

6. Keto Chicken Bowl Enchilada.

This spicy situation of chicken will leave you content until dinner time. Turn it into a rice bowl with handy dandy cauliflower rice attached.

7. Ham and Calzones Cheddar.

It's safe to assume that the calzones are likely a no-go if you follow the keto diet. That is not a typical calzone, though. It's made from almond flour, coconut flour, and whey protein, and it's stuffed with ham and melted cheese.

8. Avocado Salad with Bacon.

Get this amazing egg salad with your avocado fillings! Eat it for a more hearty meal on a bed of greens!

9. Avocado Salad at the Tuna.

Oh, hey, it's avocado again along with sliced cucumber, red onion, coriander, lemon juice, and tuna (the protein punch you need to get to your next meal). Considering the high-fat, low-carbon (and incredibly popular) keto diet is based on beef, plant-based fats, cheese, and eggs (nuts! avocado!), it's easy to pack flavourful and full keto-friendly lunches. Who needs sandwiches when you have chips with the bacon?

Turkey-Cheddar Roll-Ups

lightly-sliced turkey stands in for the tortilla in these super-simple cheese wraps. Change up the cheese throughout the week — we especially like cheddar, provolone, and dill Havarti.

Get a recipe: Roll up three slices of deli turkey (we like Applegate), with three slices of cheese.
Pack with: 1/2 avocado, almonds, blueberries, cucumber slices
Net carbs: 13 grams

Hard-Boiled Egg Snack Plate

It's easy to adore the mighty hard-boiled egg. Prep ahead by steaming a big batch over the weekend, then peel and pack on weekdays with lots of salt and pepper.
Get a recipe: 2 hard-boiled eggs.

Pack with: 1/2 avocado, string cheese, French onion dip, cucumber slices
Net carbs: 9 grams

Zoodles and Meatballs

Make an easy, keto-amiable version of spaghetti and meatballs by changing in zoodles and reaching for pre-cooked meatballs.

Get a recipe: No recipe here. Just pack up three cooked chicken meatballs.

Pack with: baby bel cheese, cubed cheddar cheese, roasted almonds, Zoodles tossed with lemon juice, and olive oil.

Net carbs: 8 grams

Chicken Sausage

Pre-cooked chicken pepperoni is a fast and easy choice for a keto-approved lunch. It comes in an extremely large variety of flavors (think: spicy andouille and Italian herb), so try different throughout the week.

Get a recipe: Just pick up a parcel of cooked chicken pepperoni (like these), slice one, and pack it.

Pack with: Almonds, radishes, French onion dip, Guacamole

Net carbs: 8 grams

Pepperoni Picnic Box

Grazing is one of the smooth ways to eat keto. veggies, Pack up some meats, and cheese and assume you're dining al fresco. Plus, you'll take any pretext to eat French onion dip at lunchtime, right?

Get a recipe: No recipe here!

Pack with: Cubed cheddar cheese, 1/2 avocado, celery sticks, French onion dip, Pepperoni slices

Net carbs: 7 grams

Smoked Salmon & Cream Cheese Roll-Ups

Expanse cream cheese onto thin slices of smoked salmon to build hand-held roll-ups you'll want to kit again and again.

Get a recipe: Spread cream cheese onto cut into a portion of smoked salmon, roll them up, and slice.

Pack with: Almonds and olive oil, cucumber slices, cherry tomatoes, Zoodles tossed with lemon juice

Net carbs: 12 grams

Bacon Chips and Dip

Crispy, salty bacon chips are the lunch staple you didn't know you needed. Tear smaller slices of bacon into large pieces, bake until crisp, and then put into guacamole come lunchtime.

Get a recipe: Guacamole and Bacon chips

Pack with: Almonds, string cheese, two hard-boiled eggs

Net carbs: 7 grams

Ranch Chicken Bites

Toss juicy chicken bites with your preferred ranch dressing for a winning lunch that will make you full.

Get a recipe: Ranch chicken bites (omit the BBQ sauce and keep the ranch dressing on the side for dipping)

Pack with: Roasted broccoli (buy it from your grocery store's hot bar),
cherry tomatoes, Babybel cheese
Net carbs: 6 grams

Hot Smoked Salmon

If you haven't already gotten to know hot smoked salmon, here's your chance: It's smoky, not too salty, and flakes easily into nice big chunks.

Get a recipe: No recipe here: just flake some hot smoked salmon.

Pack with: Guacamole, roasted broccoli (buy it from your grocery store's hot bar), blueberries, almonds

Net carbs: 11 grams

Tuna Salad Lettuce Wraps

Scoop tuna salad onto hearty romaine lettuce leaves for a creamy, crisp main. Round it out with fewer salty snacks — and an extra serving of pickles.

Get a recipe: Pick up some tuna salad from the salad bar and spoon it into romaine.

Pack with: Almonds, pickles, Cubed cheddar cheese
Net carbs: 9 grams

Keto Dinner prescription That Will Make Your Life Way Easier

If you're unfamiliar with the ketogenic diet, the Atkins diet is the modern-day answer. You will follow a low-carbohydrate and high-protein diet regimen to help boost fat burning and hopefully gain more energy. Think recipes for low-carb chicken, bunless burgers, and more. Keep on reading with these recipes to stay on the right track.

Keto Cauli tots.

Sometimes, you just want to be cheese for dinner; we hear you. Such baked cauliflower tots hide in some veg for those moments. (Through Brit+Co).

Spicy Sausage and Portobello pizza's recipes.

One of the first victims of a keto diet is pizza. The carb-charged crust is a no-go for ultra-low-carb eaters. Still, there is a serious lack of any keto meal plan that does not include these baked portobello mushrooms topped with mozzarella, tomatoes, onions, and hot Italian sausage. These tasty pizza alternatives, with just six net carbs, offer some of the "keto-approved" chicken and cauliflower crusts a more natural choice.

Chicken and Prosciutto Salad with arugula and asiago

Chicken and prosciutto salad with receta Arugula and Asiago.

Salad may seem like a distinct low-carb meal for keto consumers, but you will struggle to get enough fat with your toppings unless you're intentional with them. With chicken, this salad piles on protein and rounds off with salty, savory prosciutto for a portion of food that ends up with just over seven net carbs. Need further calories? Double the chicken.

Steak with Ginger-Scallion sauce.

Steak with a Scallion-Ginger Recipe Sauce.

Grilled steak is one of the best keto meals, so switch to this umami-rich scallion and ginger sauce when you're looking for a spice boost. Fresh ginger adds the creamy pan sauce with a bit of zipping and bite. Oyster sauce is loaded with salty, funky notes on its umami. This dish features only two net carbs, leaving plenty of room for one side of loaded mashed cauliflower.

Caesar Brussels Sprouts with Almonds Salad.

Caesar Brussels Sprouts Salad with Recipe Almonds.

Brussels sprouts are the best (green) companion to a keto eater. Such low-carb vegetables are perfectly fried in ghee or roasted in flavoring oils. When shredded raw as we did for this Caesar variety, they also happen to make a hearty salad. Six net carbs yield one serving, so finish off the plate with grilled chicken, lamb, or fish.

Chicken Pan-Grilled with Chorizo Confetti.

Chicken pan-grilled in Recipe Chorizo Confetti.

One of the easiest ways, when you're looking to boost your fat numbers, is to add meaty crumbles to the meals. Chorizo, an example of fatty Mexican sausage, is a great option, especially for chicken, pork, fish, and more. Below, for a tantalizing topper for a simply grilled chicken breast, it is served with onions, carrots, and bell peppers. The whole meal has only 2.4 net carbs, and make up for one side of a spinach salad with bacon dressing or Brussels roasted sprouts.

Salmon with Pesto, Red Pepper.

Salmon with a Pesto Recipe from Red Pepper.

Keep a bottle of grilled red peppers in your refrigerator so you can whirl a simple pesto or romesco sauce together for any protein you plan. Here, this zippy sauce with bright notes of garlic and tomato paste cuts the fatty salmon. Use your remaining carbs with some grilled or roasted asparagus for a meal, with just under two net carbs per serving.

Steak Tuscan Salad.
Tuscan Steak Recipe Salad.

A great choice for a busy weekday or a calming date night, this steak salad easily comes together thanks to fast-cooking steak strips. While the steak soaks the mashed garlic paste, mix broccoli with oil and roast it for a smooth side. Grilled green beans would be a welcome addition to complementing this keto recipe. Grill them while the steak is resting until they crisp-tender.

Chicken stuffed with goat cheese.
Recipe for goat cheese-stuffed chicken.

Adding cheese is an easy way to boost flavor and improve your macros for any meal. Herby goat cheese adds fat and flavor to this simple chicken recipe while keeping the carbs low. This simple keto dish leaves room for a side of roasted cauliflower, spinach salad, or riced cauliflower sauteed with ghee and garlic, with just one gram of carbohydrates.

Lemony Shrimp Grilled Salad.
Recipe for Lemony Grilled Shrimp Salad.

In a day of keto meal plans, this zesty salad will be a welcome break from many of the fat-rich foods you eat. Large shrimp gives a healthful dose of good-for-you fats and protein, but with a few chopped avocado, feel free to boost that number. This dish has five net carbs and nearly 20 grams of fat. If the 1/3 teaspoon of sugar is a move outside your keto comfort zone, replace stevia or erythritol with it.

Roasted Red Pepper and Chicken Sausage Patties with Spinach.
Roasted Red Pepper and Chicken Spinach Sausage Patties Recipe.

Chicken patties, like crab cakes, seem harder than they are, and they're a great vessel to smear on lots of extra fat — a spicy mayo or flavored sour cream with these patties would be delicious. With just one gram of carbohydrate and less than 200 calories, for a satisfying dinner or lunch, you might quickly double that recipe. To round out the dinner, serve with a spinach salad.

Broiled salmon and asparagus with Crème Fraîche.
Crème Fraîche Salad for broiled salmon and asparagus.

Before you know it, this sheet-pan keto meal may find its way into the rotation. Salmon is one of the fat-richest fish that you can eat, but keep boosting your macros with a luscious cream Fraiche dip, a rich, thick cream type. (Imagine big whipping cream but in a dippable or spreadable version.) If you want a bit of fat-busting zing, keep a lemon wedge close by.

Flank Steak Pan-Grilled.

Recipe for Pan-grilled Flank Steak.

Flank steak is a great weekend choice for go-to keto eaters. The ultra-thin slice of beef cooks to a perfect medium or medium-rare in just minutes. Keep the protein simple but go a little extra with the dipping sauces or glazes, such as this combination of soy and mustard, which only has two grams of net carbs. The tang of the condiments is cut by heavy whipping cream; double the sauce if you want plenty to serve over a starchy side, like cauliflower rice.

Avocados stuffed with Crab.

Recipe for Crab-Stuffed Avocados.

A tangy mayonnaise with lemon and tarragon is the perfect dressing for sweet crabmeat. This keto dinner, combined with seared avocados, is a great carb bargain (one stuffed half of an avocado has only two net carbs). There's no shame in consuming a second serving of this decadent mixture if you have the carbs and calories to spare.

Blackened Chicken Salad Vinaigrette with Blue Cheese.

Blackened Chicken Salad with a Vinaigrette Blue Cheese Recipe.

When you are sick of simple chicken salads, this blackened version and funky blue cheese vinaigrette will shake things up. The spice combination is the secret to success in this dish, which has just over six net carbs. No pre-mixed option will do; for maximum flavor satisfaction, you need to make your own. For four servings of this easy salad, a scant quarter-cup of blue cheese is used, but you can add more to boost your total fat.

Mint Raita Grilled Chicken with Tandoori.

Tandoori Grilled Chicken with Recipe Mint Raita.

The potent mixture of Indian spice and tangy yogurt during a long marinade infuses the chicken with flavor. Mix it up before going to work, or if you plan on grilling for lunch, let it sit overnight. A herby raita sauce cools down the spice punch bag. Calorie-conscious eaters prefer fat-free yogurt, but keto eaters should swap it to keep the carbs down for full-fat yogurt. Serve with a mashed cauli or cauliflower rice patty. (As it is, the chicken and sauce have just over four net carbs.)

Spice-Rubbed New York Strip with Avocado-Lime Salsa
Spice-Rubbed New York Strip with Avocado-Lime Salsa Recipe

This dish will please your palate if you are prone to add guacamole or smashed avocado to just about every food you eat to get your fat numbers greater. The best addition to grilled lean New York strip steaks is an avocado salsa complete with kicky serrano chiles, strong red onion, and zesty lime juice. The whole meal has only 2.6 net carbs in it together. Mix the salsa early to mix the spices when adding the spice rub and cook the steak. Tossed in toasty ghee, serve with roasted asparagus.

Balsamic hanger steak, with parmesan and vegetables.

Balsamic steak hanger with greens and Parmesan recette.

Hanger steak is often neglected for its more popular cousin, flank steak, but this tender cut has a supreme flavor and texture with a bit of extra fat. Don't hide the beefy flavor under the toppings and fatty dressings. Instead, keep it simple for just two net carbs with a greens pillow, a salty Parm brush, and a simple oil-and-lemon dressing.

Salmon, with Guacamole Walnut-Avocado.

Salmon with Guacamole Recipe by Walnut-Avocado.

Made from toasted walnuts and extra-virgin olive oil, this guacamole serves a serious dose of healthy fats. Combine that with salmon, and this recipe adds more than 32 grams of fat for just two net carbs to your day— and that includes a side salad. Keep pinning this one to your fridge. Often, you will come back to it.

Broccoli-and-Bacon Frittatas of muffin-tin.

Recipe for Broccoli-and-Bacon Muffin-Tin Frittatas.

Have a little fun on muffin tins and the ubiquitous keto ingredient, the potato, for this quick keto dinner. When turning the modest mini frittatas into sweet snacks, you can enjoy breakfast, lunch, or dinner, and salty bacon pulls the taste punches. (For the latter two meals, just serve with salad.) Replace heavy whipping cream with reduced-fat milk to notch down the carb number. Two mini frittatas, as it is, just turn up two net carbs.

Quick Piccata Chicken.

Fast Recipe Piccata Chicken.

For keto eaters, chicken thighs are a great option because the dark meat packs more flavor and fat than ultra-lean breasts. A simple white-wine sauce gets a zingy boost from briny capers and lemon juice for those thighs which have only three net carbs. Serve to round out the meal with broccoli or a massaged kale salad.

Wraps of Asian Pork Lettuce.

Recipe for Asian Pork Lettuce Wraps.

You can have Wrap Wednesday, but You can't have Taco Tuesday, and you'll be reserving it on your calendar for weeks to come once you try out these Asian-inspired wraps. For these wraps, the umami-rich fish sauce pulls the flavor weight; it is combined with serrano chile, ginger, garlic, and a bit of vinegar for mouth-tingling pork sauce. Three ample wraps produce only two net carbs. This is a bargain on carb!

Salisbury Steak and Gravy of Mushroom.

Salisbury Steak, with Gravy Recipe Mushroom.

At its best, this is keto comfort food. This Salisbury steak, with just over five net carbs, is draped in a luscious mushroom gravy made with red wine, beef broth, and butter. The sauce often calls for one teaspoon of all-purpose flour as a thickener, which is seldom available in keto pantries. Never be afraid: Replace the almond flour if you don't have it or don't want to use it.

Flaky Crab Cakes.
Simple Recipe for Flaky Crab Cakes.

Don't overestimate how long crab cakes take to make. Keeping the mix simple and sticky will help the cakes easily come together and cook fast. Two of these cakes are just five net carbs, so serve with a side salad doused in a lemon dressing, and scoop up an Old Bay mayo for a coastal dinner that meets your keto requirements.

Halibut sauteed with Romesco sauce.
Halibut sauteed in Romesco sauce recette.

Here's another perfect reason to keep roasted red peppers bottled in your fridge. Romesco sauce is an almond, oil, and vinegar creamy pepper sauce and whirled up in the blender. It adds a bright, tangy flavor to any protein; here, it's served with sauteed halibut for just seven net carbs. Smoky ancho is not always used in romesco sauces, but in this fish dish, it is a welcome contrast.

Chicken Breasts grilled with satay sauce.
Grilled Chicken Breasts with Recipe Satay Sauce.

Whenever you can add a sauce rich in fat to lean protein, do so. Keto eaters are one of the best ways to keep their macro-counts in order. Here the simple grilled chicken breasts get a satay taste and fat lift, an Asian-inspired nut butter sauce with vinegar and chili sauce bursts of flavor. Just six net carbs are on the final dish. The chicken spice rub has a bit of brown sugar; you can look for a keto-friendly alternative or eliminate it.

Pork Loin Filled with Spinach cheese and goat cheese.

Pork Loin Filled with Spinach Recipe and Goat Cheese.

This stuffed pork loin dish is part of a holiday dinner or special occasion, but it's so decadent that your friends won't know it's keto. It's a slow cooker keto meal as a treat so you can concentrate on making other sides and having the house ready while this cooks. Apricot preserves are low in sugar, and there are only six net carbs per serving in the final dish, so don't think about a replacement here. Serve with roasted broccoli or grilled asparagus. (Your guests may have the mashed potatoes.) Horseradish Butter grilled flank steak.

Grilled flank steak with Horseradish butter

Grilled flank steak with Horseradish butter recipe.
If you haven't found out about the secret of compound butter, it's time now. In this fast dish, which has only

one net carb, the Tangy horseradish kicks up simple flank steak. Make extra butter from horseradish; you'll surely find plenty of ways to use it once you have your first taste. Serve Pulled Pork Lettuce Wraps with a side of sauteed or creamed spinach.

Pulled pork lettuce wraps

Recipe for pulled pork lettuce wraps.

While sugar is used here for the pork in the initial rub, there are only four net carbs on the final dish. Don't hesitate to kill him. The often-tough pork shoulder becomes juicy and soft with a low-and-slow roast in the oven. The pulled pork is finally tossed in a mixture of sweet-spicy gochujang, soy sauce, and ginger. What's more, the leftovers just get better as the pork soaks up the sauce over food.

Chicken larb.

Recipe for Chicken Larb.

A food processor breaks down chicken breasts into tiny pieces, soaking up this larb's curry and chile flavors faster. Everything also cooks in just 10 minutes, so you can make this keto meal in less than 30 minutes, and just under four net carbs.

Kale and Mushroom Frittata.

Kale and Mushroom Frittata Recipe.

Frittatas are a great clean-out - the-fridge choice for keto eaters. Toss leftover meat, vegetables, and cheese into an egg and cream base for a quick and effective dinner. If you don't have the leftovers and still want to try this versatile dish, kale and mushrooms are ideal for a keto-friendly frittata, which will both tenderize and become sweeter and toastier in the baking process. You can eat this at breakfast, or for lunch or dinner with grilled veggies or salad.

Italian Chicken Sausage and Soup with Artichoke.

Italian Chicken Sausage and Soup with Artichoke Recipe.

This basic soup is a wonderful make-ahead keto meal choice, with just over three grams of net carbs. Spanish chicken sausage imbues the chicken broth with fennel and herb flavors. Spinach is silky in the heat of the broth, and artichoke hearts, a normal but fully keto-friendly substitute, are tooth-some and chewy without waxy. If you need a bit of crunch, skip the ciabatta bread and eat with keto crackers.

Sizzling Skirt Steak with Red Pepper and Asparagus.
Sizzling Asparagus Skirt Steak with Red Pepper Recipe.

This quick keto dinner is a great option for busy weeknights, for just five ingredients and seven net carbs. Fish sauce is potent enough in a short period to add significant flavor. In a false stir-fry, asparagus and onion both tenderize easily. Don't just crowd out the pan. If your pan is too small, then everything will steam or boil instead of fry.

Chicken Breasts in Greek-style.

Chicken Breasts in Greek-style Recipe.

Briny olives and tangy feta cheese, both excellent sources of fat, form the flavourful basis for chicken breasts of this Greek-inspired topper. Another fast-cooking keto meal, this dish has only six net carbs, so you have room for a salad or broil vegetables on the side.

A Sample Keto Meal Plan For 1 Week

To help get you along, here is a case ketogenic diet meal plan for one week:

Monday

Breakfast: Tomatoes, eggs, and Bacon.
Lunch: Cheese with olive oil and feta Chicken salad.

Dinner: Asparagus cooked in butter with Salmon.

Tuesday

Breakfast: Goat cheese omelet, basil, and egg, tomato.

Lunch: Milk share, peanut butter, cocoa powder, and stevia Almond milk.

Dinner: Vegetables, cheddar cheese, and Meatballs.

Wednesday

Breakfast: A ketogenic milkshake.

Lunch: Avocado with olive oil and Shrimp salad.

Dinner: Broccoli, salad, and Pork chops with Parmesan cheese.

Thursday

Breakfast: Salsa, peppers, onion, spices, and Omelet with avocado.

Lunch: Guacamole, salsa with a handful of nuts and celery sticks.

Dinner: Vegetables, along with Chicken stuffed with pesto and cream cheese.

Friday

Breakfast: Cocoa powder, stevia, and Sugar-free yogurt with peanut butter.

Lunch: Vegetables with Beef stir-fry cooked in coconut oil.

Dinner: Egg, cheese with Bun-less burger with bacon.

Saturday

Breakfast: Vegetables with Ham and cheese omelet.

Lunch: Nuts with Ham and cheese slices.

Dinner: Whitefish and egg, with Spinach cooked in coconut oil.

Sunday

Breakfast: Fried eggs and Mushroom with bacon.

Lunch: Guacamole, cheese, and Burger with salsa.

Dinner: Side salad with Steak and eggs.

Always try to change the vegetables and meat over the long term, as each type gives different nourishment and health benefits.

Healthy Keto Snacks

In case you get hungry amidst meals, here are some healthful, keto-approved snacks:

Cheese with olives

1–2 hard-boiled eggs

A handful of nuts or seeds

Fatty meat or fish

Cheese

90% dark chocolate

A low-carb milkshake with nut butter, cocoa powder, and almond milk

Full-fat yogurt mixed with cocoa powder and nut butter

Smaller portions of leftover meals

Celery with salsa and guacamole

Strawberries and cream

Great snacks for a keto diet include boiled eggs, cheese, olives, pieces of meat, nuts, and dark chocolate.

Additives to a Ketogenic Diet.

Although no additional supplements are needed, some may be useful.

MCT oil: MCT oil is added to drinks or yogurt, providing energy and helping to increase ketone levels.

Minerals: Due to water and mineral balance shifts, salt added and other minerals may be necessary before beginning.

Caffeine: Caffeine can bring energy, fat loss, and performance benefits.

Exogenous ketones: This treatment helps elevate ketone levels in the body.

Creatine: The health and performance benefits of creatine are numerous. That can help if you combine exercise with a ketogenic diet.

Whey: To boost your daily protein intake, use half a scoop of whey protein in shakes or yogurt.

Conclusion

Although short-term benefits for people, including weight loss and increases in blood sugar and blood pressure have been shown by ketogenic diet trials, the jury is still out on whether such effects can be replicated over the long term.

"The ketogenic diet has the ability to be a game-changer." Still, a lot depends on whether its effects propagate across large-scale studies and whether people can withstand long-term nutritional restrictions. People who are striving to lose weight for health reasons should keep it on their radar and stay tuned for the process. "It is important to reduce your carb intake significantly initially. You can eat carbs again on special occasions after the first 2–3 months but stick to eating shortly afterward.

You're going to lose weight, but on any diet, there's a risk of losing any muscle. Nevertheless, the high intake of protein and high levels of ketone will help minimize muscle loss, particularly if you lift weights. Protein should be modest on the keto diet since very high doses will increase insulin levels and lower ketones. The upper limit is potentially around 35 percent of the total calorie intake. You may not be in total ketosis, or use fats and ketones efficiently. To counter that, however, lower your carb intake and revisit the above points. A medication such as MCT oil or ketones may benefit too. As digestion problems and diarrhea, there is a common side effect but usually passes after 3–4 weeks. If this persists, try eating more veggies with high fiber. Magnesium supplements can also be of assistance with constipation.

For people who are diabetic, overweight, or looking to improve their metabolic health, a ketogenic diet can be great. It may be less appropriate for elite athletes or those who wish to add large amounts of weight or muscle. So, as with any diet, it will only succeed if you are disciplined over the long term, so adhere to it. That said, few things in nutrition are as well-proven as the powerful benefits of a ketogenic diet in terms of health and weight loss.

CPSIA information can be obtained
at www.ICGtesting.com
Printed in the USA
BVHW051126110321
602311BV00010B/534